W9-CHZ-927

Chapel Hill 1986
(from Anne Stapleton) Samuel

Mom, Can We Still Keep Roger?

SURVIVAL GUIDE FOR MOTHERS OF PRESCHOOLERS

FREDA INGLE BRIGGS

BAKER BOOK HOUSE
Grand Rapids, Michigan 49506

Copyright 1985 by Baker Book House

ISBN: 0-8010-0888-3

Laurie Sienkowski, Illustrator

Scripture quotations not otherwise identified are from the Revised Standard Version of the Holy Bible, © 1946, 1952 by Division of Christian Education of the National Council of the Churches of Christ in the United States of America. Scripture quotations identified KJV are from the King James Version.

Printed in the United States of America

For my husband and children
and those who don't know when to call it quits

Contents

Introduction

Somewhere between family planning and women's lib, motherhood as a career has slipped to the status of noble pastime. You know what I mean. You're nine-and-a-half months pregnant, pushing two whining toddlers in the grocery cart, and you get the "Doesn't she know what causes that?" look.

When I told one friend that I suspected my third pregnancy, she turned down the corners of her mouth and said, "Maybe you can do something about that next time."

When Linda's fourth child was on the way, she told one woman who made such a fuss about it, "Well, I *am* married, you know!"

Believe me, I now tell each pregnant friend and acquaintance how happy I am for her, no matter how many children she already has, or how young the oldest one is. She needs all the support she can get.

That's what this book is about. I just want to give a little support to moms of several young children, or what may just seem to be several. As my mother says, "You might as well have six. Even one takes up all of your time. Six couldn't take up any more."

Psalm 127:3, 5 says: "Lo, sons are a heritage from the LORD. . . . Happy is the man who has his quiver full of

7

them!" Do you know that there are five arrows in a quiver? My dear husband will have to find some other way to be happy.

With family planning so sophisticated, it seems that no woman would have to have two children in diapers at the same time. I know that having three children under five is not so unusual, and you can probably top me with how close in age your own children are, but most think such fertility unnecessary.

One older gentleman says, "What's all this fuss about family planning? We planned for each of ours six months before they were born."

Most of this book was written while our sons, Bruce, Roger, and Alex, were five, three, and one. (This accounts for my rare use of the pronouns *she* or *her*. But the ideas apply to either gender.) I knew that if I waited any longer to put down my thoughts, I would forget what it was really like to prepare supper with one child clinging to my leg and two others crying in the living room.

The women whose names I use in this book are either in the throes of rearing their young children or have lived to tell about it. I often hear two phrases passed around—"I don't know how you do it," and "You do what you have to do."

A friend and I were talking after church one Sunday about names for the baby. She was pregnant with her fourth, I with my third. An older woman walked by and, hearing the topic of our conversation, said, "I know what you ought to call it. You ought to call it 'Quits!'"

This book is for those who don't know when to call it quits.

1

The Joy of Coping

The Joy of Coping

If you are reading this book, you probably have it propped open with your elbow while spooning Gerber's finest off your baby's face and into his mouth. You've just had another dry run at the potty chair with your toddler, and your preschooler is practicing using scissors by cutting in half the coupons you so carefully clipped.

Somehow, when that man you married mentioned something about being "the mother of my children," he imparted a little more hearts and flowers, moonlight, and serenade to the suggestion.

My mother says they should give children the tranquilizers and mothers the vitamins. This bit of insight comes from the time in her life when she had three children under four years of age. Dad says he never knew who he would find crying when he came home—Mom or one of the kids.

When I started having babies, I promised myself I would be bright enough not to do as my mother did. "All I was, was a mother!" she says. No wonder she cried when she found out number four was on the way, having just taken number three out of diapers. When the fifth one came along, it didn't seem to make that much difference.

If you are feeling like "just a mother" these days, here are a few suggestions to help you cope with life with little ones:

1. Have a hobby. This hobby, however, must be something that can be done standing up and in the kitchen. Sitting down to a project triggers an instant "Mo-mm-my!" that starts from the far corners of the house and usually ends up in the kitchen. Start supper while you are there.

2. Eat out at least once a week. Bologna sandwiches taste the same on the back porch as they would at the finest restaurant in town.

3. Read. *The Little Engine That Could* is a very inspiring story.

4. Subscribe to a magazine other than Sears' Christmas catalog.

5. Change your name. If you are tired of hearing "Mommy!" all day, this is a simple solution. No one has to know that you will answer only to "Phoebe" or "Alexandria."

6. Do something for yourself. This is the romanticized notion of curling up with a good book on a rainy day. In reality it means shaving your legs or taking a bath without an audience.

7. Change into something soft and slinky before your husband gets home. Then hold the baby at arm's length.

8. If your husband wonders what you do all day, tell him, "I watch TV and eat bonbons." He'd never believe the truth.

No matter how covered with crayon the walls are, how deep the piles of spilled cereal, or what the baby does in his pants as you are dashing out the door, moms somehow cope.

When little voices join yours in singing "Jesus Loves Me," when the baby first learns to kiss and wants to use your face as target practice, when your difficult toddler hugs your legs and declares, "My sweet Mommy" in the middle of a trying day, you know that your children are making your world a better place.

We do the best we can for them, because the individuals they are becoming will also make the world a better place for others.

And besides, chasing children burns calories.

2

One Step Ahead

One Step Ahead

Gayle has two adopted daughters, one four years, the other six months. Although the doctors have said it would be medically impossible, Gayle just found out that she is pregnant.

Debbi has three little boys who were once all under five years. Debbi just gave birth to a baby girl and is doing the three-under-five routine all over again. The oldest boy is now six.

Nancy is involved in all the activities of her nine- and ten-year-old son and daughter, plus various committees of her own. She is thirty-eight years old and also has two other daughters, ages one and two. Nancy is pregnant again.

I have just met Susan. She says she is finally able to get out of the house, having gone through twelve years of diapers. Susan is a mother of five boys and one girl, ages two through twelve, stepmother of two, and neighborhood favorite of many.

Kay's three are all three and under. Patti's three are three and under, and so are Kathy's. Nancy S.'s five are eight and under.

Now hear this, mothers of young children! The number-one thing you can do for yourself and your family is to keep physically fit. I do not mean that you must try to look as sleek and svelte as Lady Di (poor girl—she married a prince and everyone insists on calling her "Lady"). You do not even need to be thin. But you do need to guard your health like the crown jewels.

Your children need you to be physically fit. You are at their constant demand for everything from changing diapers and pulling up training pants to dashing across the house when you hear a crash and a cry, not to mention marathon nighttime teething sessions.

After Alex, our third son, was born, my mother-in-law came to help out for "just a few days," which turned into a few weeks. I just couldn't pull myself out of a physical slump. Even after the baby was sleeping all night, I was waking up in the morning every bit as tired as I had been when I went to bed.

I kept hearing, "Well, you're breast-feeding," or, "Well, you have those other children to look after," or (this is my favorite), "Well, you are a little older."

The obvious solution was exercise.

Now, I like to exercise about as much as I like to scrape gum off the bottom of a sneaker. In fact, having babies is the perfect excuse not to exercise. Don't most doctors say to take it easy for six weeks after the baby is born? That's six weeks of guilt-free "Don't strain yourself."

Jane Fonda is about to ruin this for all of us. Women come to her famous after-baby workouts with their two-week-old infants. Check with your doctor to get his or her opinion about exercise for you.

Every once in a while I go through a physical-fitness craze. My last one was in college, twelve years ago. I even bought a pair of fancy running shoes. The original shoe-strings are still in place.

This time, though, my motivation for exercise was running high. I simply had to feel better. I trained Don to roust me out of bed by 6:30 A.M., so I could get in fifteen minutes of bend-and-stretch with a local TV expert. Believe me, it's not easy to do jumping jacks in a flannel nightgown.

15

After I have been stretched and somewhat aerobicized (a quarter-hour TV show doesn't allow much time for puffing and panting), I gulp down a handful of vitamins. "Oh, oh," you say, "she's one of those."

While certainly no nutrition expert, I have done some research and encourage you to do the same. Remember that everybody is different, and what seems to work for me may not be just right for you.

Take something good for your nervous system. Do you know of any mother of young children who does not need help in this department? Brewer's yeast and B vitamins fall into this category.

Take calcium supplements. Most of us need more than we are getting from the food we eat. Calcium is good bone insurance, can aid in giving you a good night's sleep—provided the children sleep through—and can help eliminate all those little undefined aches and pains.

Take liver tablets, such as dessicated liver, for the iron you may be missing in your diet. Consuming adequate amounts of complete protein is also essential in combating fatigue. Show me a mother of young children who is not tired, and I'll show you a household expense account that includes a governess.

Take vitamin E "just because." Pay attention now. Vitamin E slows aging, protects red blood cells, prevents blood clots (important after childbirth), maintains healthy muscles and nerves, is good for hair, skin, and mucuos membranes. If you have a friend who is having trouble getting pregnant, recommend that both she and her husband take a vitamin E supplement, since deficiency symptoms include sterility, impotency, and miscarriages. In her book *God and Vitamins*, Marjorie Holmes describes vitamin E as the vitamin for youth, heart, and energy. Hooray!

Take vitamin C because it helps you fight some infections. If you want to stave off the viruses going around, including the common cold, check into what vitamin C can do for you. I know there are those who say all vitamin C will do is give you expensive urine. I want to tell you, though, that whenever I feel even the slightest hint of a sore throat or other cold symptoms coming on, I double up on the vitamin C, and those symptoms soon disappear. We all know a mom is not allowed to get sick. Prevention is the secret.

Vitamins and minerals are dependent on each other in order to do their job properly. That's why a balanced diet is so important, but also why I take a few supplements. I am never sure of getting enough of everything I need from the food I eat.

The owner of our town's health-food store, who had five children in six years and lived to tell the tale, says that a well-nourished mother can put up with a husband who rarely (or never) helps out. Well, that's another chapter, but it says it all about taking care of ourselves.

Back to exercise. After changing into appropriate clothes, I head out the door for a brisk fifteen- or twenty-minute walk, weather cooperating. If it's cold, I run-walk. If the forecast is for an over-100° day, I take it easy. Why ruin the coolest part of the day by sweating?

I usually get back before the kids wake up, giving me time to shower, dress, and maybe stick a piece of bread in the toaster. This routine cranks me up and keeps me one step ahead of the troops.

It's so much better than awakening to the sound of the baby's crying, the feel of the toddler's wet training pants, and the exuberance of a preschooler who yanks off my covers and says, "Time to get up, Mommy! I want Cheerios for breakfast and I already tried to pour my milk!"

You may think you're getting enough bend-and-stretch at the clothesline by hanging up dozens of miniature socks; plenty of weight-lifting by carting the diaper pail from the changing table to the laundry room; and sufficient jogging from chasing kids away from the edge of the street. But every "Doctor, why do I feel so tired?" article I've ever read features a dragged-out mother of preschoolers. The doctor says, "Get some exercise." The mother says, "Doctor, you've got to be kidding!" (Maybe you also used that line the last time you discovered you were pregnant.)

The truth of the matter is that to really feel good and make your body work for you, aerobic exercise is necessary. This simply means doing something that pumps oxygen into your bloodstream and to your brain. I'm in favor of anything that keeps my brain from turning to mush.

Aerobics can take the form of brisk walking, jogging, swimming, jumping rope, bicycling, gym-type workouts, or the all-time favorite, aerobic dancing. A young mother in our church has been trained to teach aerobics to the tunes of gospel music.

Ron and Jeannie worked an aerobic dance class into their already tight budget. Ron says that the money spent was the best investment he ever made. Jeannie felt better, was happier with herself, and was able to deal with the family more calmly and effectively.

If your self-esteem is suffering, start on an exercise program. You can bend and stretch to a record in your own living room, or join an organized group for bowling, volleyball, tennis, or whatever. You'll feel better mentally and physically.

The harried-housewife syndrome exists because of fatigue and depression. Exercise is a proven mood-lifter. Dr. Robert S. Brown of the University of Virginia School of Medicine says, "Exercise produces chemical and psychological changes that improve your mental health."[2] Here again, aerobic exercise is the key—at least three times a week for a minimum of about fifteen minutes.

But any exercise is better than no exercise. And if it's good for you, it's good for your children. You'll feel better about yourself and your ability to cope with your youngsters. My baby's favorite entertainment is to watch me do windmills in front of his high chair. He loves the motion. If there's an exercise program on TV while the older children are awake, let them watch, and encourage them to participate with you. They will enjoy trying to duplicate what they see, and it's good for their coordination. Or you can put on a record and have them take turns being the exercise leader.

My exercise program this time around has been a success because my goal has not been to lose weight or firm up acres of flab. My goal has been simply to feel better. And I do feel better. The tired-mama look has disappeared. The color has returned to my cheeks.

There are still a few skeptics to convince that I'm serious about this thing. "Look!" I blurted out one morning to my husband, "I can touch my nose to my knees!"

"What happened," he asked, "did your nose grow?"

Notes

1. Marjorie Holmes, *God and Vitamins* (New York: Avon Books, 1982), pp. 248, 249.

2. Joan R. Heilman, "Six Self-Help Tips to Rout the Blues," *Reader's Digest,* December 1983 (from *Family Circle,* July 12, 1983).

3

Spiritual Fitness

Spiritual Fitness

Does your spiritual life consist of sitting in a church pew on Sunday morning, out of breath and hoping that the Lord can forgive you for the screaming and yelling that took place just moments before? You finally found all of the shoes; two of the children have socks that don't match—no matter, they're hidden under pant legs; your daughter kept pulling the barrettes out of her hair; and the baby did everything in his pants that he could possibly do, just as you opened the front door to leave.

As you take a deep breath your husband leans over to you and whispers, "Did you mean to wear those earrings?"

"Yes, why?"

"They don't match."

Kathy M. says one of her daughters shocked her into doing something about the Sunday-morning madness when she said, "You can sure tell it's Sunday morning by the way Mom is screaming."

There are two things you can do to avoid such scenes. The first thing is to prepare physically. Get ready for Sunday morning on Saturday. Lay out the clothes. Do the mending. Prepare two outfits for yourself. Change purses Saturday, pack the diaper bag Saturday, and then plan an uncomplicated breakfast and a simple lunch for Sunday.

Nothing ruins Sunday more than coming home to

heavy K.P. duty after a lovely morning of worship. The kids are hungry and tired, but your husband expects a traditional Sunday dinner. Either crock-pot a casserole meal while you are all at church (prepared the night before), have leftovers, or train your husband to eat tuna-fish sandwiches for lunch after church. The latter works best for us, so I prepare a more substantial meal for the evening. We also enjoy the unofficial tradition of occasionally bringing home a large pizza with everything on it from a pizza parlor conveniently located on our way home from church.

The second thing you can do is prepare mentally. Get out of your church pew and into the Word daily. I don't mean that you should stop going to church on Sunday morning, but that you need to exercise your spiritual muscles more than once a week. Don't be a weekend spiritual athlete.

Seek the fellowship of believers. From my perch in the choir loft, I can look around and count the couples I would love to see in Sunday school. It's not that they haven't been invited, or that no one has shown an interest in them. Perhaps they are fearful of new situations, or maybe they came once a long time ago and "didn't get anything out of it" or were inadvertently offended. Or they may be afraid someone will ask them to read or pray out loud.

Some couples (and individuals) never attend the Wednesday-night supper and Bible study or other programs and activities offered by our church. In fact, the new faces in our fellowships usually come from new members—not the Sunday-morning-only faces who finally decide it's time to step out and grow.

Well, I've just inspired myself to make a few phone calls to some of those old faces. And I hope that if you are a church-pew warmer, you will take some steps to become a church-body warmer. Believe me, there are people in Bible studies, Sunday school, women's groups, and other church programs who would love to say to you, "Oh, I'm so glad to see you here!"

Seek the fellowship of God through his Word. You don't have time to read the Bible? Nonsense! You don't have time not to! Think of the time wasted and aggravation spent on a project for which you didn't read the instructions. God didn't send you these children without leaving you an instruction manual. Read it!

If you are not in the habit (or have fallen out of the habit) of daily Bible reading, whet your spiritual appetite with daily readings from a devotional book. Start in the New Testament with a chapter a day. Read a Psalm daily. My mother says one of the biggest spiritual boosts she had was reading the entire Book of Psalms in one week. Commit to memory the verses with Scripture references that your children bring home from their Sunday-school lessons. Read Bible stories to the children each day, remembering not to let this be a substitute for your own study. Buy a fill-in-the-blanks Bible-study booklet from a Christian bookstore. Make a daily goal of a certain number of questions to finish. Write down in a notebook any new insights you receive from your reading, or copy a verse that particularly applies to your situation.

Starting out, or restarting, as the case may be, with these appetizers from God's Word will create a hunger that only more time with God can fill. If the extent of your prayer life is "Please, God, let the baby go back to sleep," it's time to plug in to the powerful combination of Bible study and prayer.

My mother jokes, "The devil invented permanent press!" In the days when everything needed ironing, Mom prayed at the ironing board. But when permanent press came along, this household altar was put away, except for an occasional sleeve or a shirt that had lain crumpled in the bottom of the dryer for several days.

My best time for prayer is during my early-morning walks. The oxygen is just starting to pump through my body; I'm alone and feel exhilarated. "O Lord, our Lord, how majestic is thy name in all the earth! Thou whose glory above the heavens is chanted by the mouths of babes and infants. . ." (Ps. 8:1–2).

Marie, mother of five, starts her day with prayer. Verletta, whose adopted children were two years old and sixteen months old when a son was born to them, says that when the children were young she would often come to the Throne of Grace at the toilet.

Kathy says that she must have a daily quiet time. She meditates on what the day will be, sets her daily goals, then accepts the fact that things won't always happen as planned. Their third son is a "special care" infant with heart and lung problems. Having this baby has helped her to be able to "give it all" to the Lord.

Ann Ortlund says in *Disciplines of the Beautiful Woman,* "A mother of small children gets a dozen unpleasant surprises a day! She needs time to settle her heart with God and be a growing Christian."[1]

She describes her hunger for the Lord when her children were ages two and a half, one and a half, and newborn. She prayed, "Lord, if you'll help me, I'll meet you from two to three A.M." And she did: "I kept my tryst with Him until the schedule lightened; I didn't die, and I'm not sorry I did it. Everybody has twenty-four hours. We can soak ourselves in prayer, in His Word, in Himself, if we really want to."[2]

The Lord has given us guidelines for prayer. These have been put into an acronym that many people use in their quiet time: ACTS—Adoration, Confession, Thanksgiving, Supplication.

He wants our praise, our adoration. "Sing praises to God, sing praises! Sing praises to our King, sing praises!" (Ps. 47:6). "For it is written, 'As I live, says the Lord, every knee shall bow to me, and every tongue shall give praise to God'" (Rom. 14:11).

God also wants us to confess our sins. "If we confess our sins, he is faithful and just, and will forgive our sins and cleanse us from all unrighteousness" (1 John 1:9). It's a lot easier for me to confess personal-type sins than sins I have committed as a mother. I feel so low in God's sight about those times when I yell at the kids irrationally, or when I dare not spank because my anger is so overwhelming I'm afraid I may hurt a child, or when I do not spend the time with them that they require. But the Lord takes me in his forgiving arms, and I know that I'm still his child and that he is helping me. When we do the best we can as parents and "train up a child in the way he should go . . ." we should leave in God's hands the part about ". . . and when he is old he will not depart from it" (Prov. 22:6).

Galatians 6:9 says, "And let us not grow weary in well-doing, for in due season we shall reap, if we do not lose heart." Dear mothers, confess your sins, your doubts, your fears, your anger, and your frustrations to the Lord. He understands and forgives. Now forgive yourself. And do not lose heart.

Over and over, from Old Testament to New, we are told to give thanks to God. "It is good to give thanks to the Lord . . ." (Ps. 92:1), and "always and for everything [give] thanks in the name of our Lord Jesus Christ to God the Father" (Eph. 5:20). Not only are we to give thanks, but we are to be thankful for all things: "Give thanks in all circumstances; for this is the will of God in Christ Jesus for you" (1 Thess. 5:18).

I used to ignore the part about giving thanks in *all* things. If I got a flat tire, how could I be expected to jump out of the car and say, "Praise the Lord!"? But as I grow in my Christian life, I know that giving thanks in all circumstances will lead to the peace that Christ offers.

"Thank you, God, for screaming children. Without them I would be so lonely and sad."

"Thank you that the baby wakes up in the middle of the night. It gives us some cuddle time together."

"Thank you that my husband is such a good provider and hard worker even though he isn't here as much as we need him."

"I don't know why this has happened, Lord, but I thank you for your perfect timing and pray you will use this situation to your honor and glory."

Be in the habit of thanking God aloud and often for your children. Grab a grubby hand and say, "Thank you, God, for Tara." Or, "Oh, God, I'm so thankful we have Jaymee." I had been in the habit of saying out loud, "Thank you, God, for Bruce," as I dropped him off at school or as he left to walk with friends. One day as he got out of the car, I forgot, but Roger stuck his head out the window and yelled, "Thank you, God, for Bruce!"

God wants us to come to him with requests. Asking—coming to the Lord with supplication—helps me relax. A popular Christian song has the words, "You gotta be laid back. . . . Simmerin' way back in His love." That's how it is when we can lay our physical, emotional, and spiritual needs at the Master's feet. I also know that the Lord can change my ideas about what I need, as he did when I quit my teaching job and was afraid of "losing my identity."

Be prepared for God's creative answers to prayer. I used to pray for patience, and he gave me three children on whom to practice my patience. "Ask, and it will be given you . . ." (Matt. 7:7).

The command, "Pray without ceasing" (1 Thess. 5:17, KJV), has a special meaning to mothers that it can have to no one else. It means that my Partner in childrearing is closer than the next cry of "Mommy!"

I have learned not always to make it a silent prayer when I come to the Lord with quick requests or items of praise. Bobbie told about a time she lost her keys. When she found them, her two-year-old daughter went over to a picture of Jesus on the wall and said, "Thank you, Jesus." Bobbie told this as a cute story about her daughter, but I thought, *Now there's a mom who has taught her daughter that God cares about our everyday needs.* Without a doubt, Bobbie had been in the habit of vocal prayer and praise in her home.

The goal, Mom, is not just to have a worshipful experience on Sunday morning, but to worship every day. Relax. Know that the Lord is bigger than any problem you have. "And my God will supply every need of yours according to his riches in Christ Jesus" (Phil. 4:19).

Claim God's promises by exercising your spiritual muscles.

Notes

1. Anne Ortlund, *Disciplines of the Beautiful Woman* (Waco, Texas: Word Books, 1981), p. 69.

2. *Ibid.*, p. 29.

4

We Are Not Having a Good Day

We Are Not Having
a Good Day

One summer day my husband came home for lunch and found me standing in the middle of the kitchen floor screaming, "I'm sick of these kids! I'm sick of this house! I've just had it!"

He tossed me that "poor fool" look and said in his irritatingly calm voice, "Why don't you turn on the air conditioner?"

Paul says in Romans 14:19, "Let us then pursue what makes for peace and for mutual upbuilding."

Paul wrote these words with the church at Rome in mind, but if it was good enough for the Romans, it's good enough for my home. Heat makes me crazy. If I turn on the air conditioner fairly early in the day, my home will likely be more peaceful.

Pursuing peace! What a task the Lord has given mothers of little ones!

I have been known to arrive at meetings with a deep sigh, clenched teeth, and the explanation, "We are not having a good day." You know what? I don't do that anymore— not because I quit going to meetings, although it has been helpful to cut down on outside activities, and not because we no longer have our bad moments. The reason is that I have learned to roll with the punches. Work that motto in cross-stitch and hang it above your kitchen sink: ROLL

WITH THE PUNCHES. Relax. Expect the unexpected. Don't take yourself or your situation so seriously.

Here's one "punch" to roll with, and I consider it an unwritten law of motherhood: your children most need attention when you are least able to give it to them.

I can easily leave a sinkful of dishes in favor of *The Cat in the Hat* when the request is, "Mommy, book, please."

"All right, Sweetie, just let me dry my hands."

But if the baby is eating graham-cracker crumbs from the kitchen floor, the toddler is whining and wiping his nose on my pant leg, and the preschooler is pounding the piano keys, the dishes suddenly become the most important thing in the world, and I become increasingly frustrated and agitated because those kids just won't let me get my work done!

Sometimes the need for attention is obvious and easily met: a pacifier in the mouth (the baby's, not mine), a shoe to be tied, a big hug and kiss, a cracker in the hand. Be prepared for those more intense situations. A repertoire of "Stop! Hold everything" activities will help you roll with the punches.

When I say, "Okay, guys, let's make cookies," our troubles are over—unless I'm out of brown sugar.

Marching around the coffee table to music is a good diversion. If you are brave, bring out the wooden spoons and pan lids. For a quieter parade, use lids from your plastic mixing bowls.

Or load everyone up for a drive in the car. Maybe they'll fall asleep. You can also take a walk, read a book, color with them in their coloring books, draw pictures for them to chuckle over ("This is Daddy when he was a baby." Tee-hee-hee!), play in the sandbox. . . .

Humor works, too. Do something silly to break the tension. Terri and her youngsters take a smile break. "Soon everyone is giggling," she says. Or muster up a twinkle in your eye and "warn" your child, "Don't you dare laugh." Keep up the joke until you are all laughing and hugging.

You know those funny faces you made to get the baby to laugh? The older kids still like them, especially if accompanied by a silly voice. Sing a silly song. I hate to admit it, but "Little Bunny Phoo-Phoo" often has a more calming effect than "Jesus Loves Me."

Denise says, "I just act like they act. If I get down on the floor and throw a tantrum, it's not long before they're all rolling in laughter instead of anger."

Recite fractured nursery rhymes: "Sing a song of sixpence, a pocket full of worms . . ." or "Little Miss Muffett sat on a toadstool. . . ." Put a record on the wrong speed on the record player—they'll forget their troubles in no time.

Laughter is healthy, no doubt about it. Think about your verbal reactions to your children. Are you doing more yelling—or more laughing? Which creates the least amount of stress? "A cheerful heart is a good medicine, but a downcast spirit dries up the bones" (Prov. 17:22). In your next quiet time look up Proverbs 15:13 and Proverbs 15:15. Laughter, indeed, is the best medicine.

In fact, when all three little ones are crying at once, all I can do is have an attitude of laughter. The chaos conjures up that picture I once saw: a whole brood of little bunnies, kicking, shoving, pushing, screaming (got the idea?), and Mama Bunny sitting serenely in her rocking chair—inside of the playpen.

Serenity. Create for yourself a little island of peace. If you spend a lot of time at the kitchen sink, place around the area things you enjoy looking at—a beautiful plant, a fresh flower, favorite knickknack, a picture of a peaceful scene.

Do you have a corner where you can retreat? Perhaps it's a favorite chair with books and magazines handy. Everyone needs his or her own spot. Observe your children as they pick out a favorite place in the house.

And, in the midst of chaos, create an island of peace within yourself. Those times that I cried right along with the baby, I also sobbed, "Thank you, God. Thank you for the beautiful gift of these children. Thank you, thank you, thank you, God . . ." over and over and out loud, until his peace filled me. That's praise therapy, and it works. "Pursuing peace" means calming your spirit.

I commented once to my friend Linda that she seemed to have so much patience with her four children. She smiled and said, "What choice do I have?" Peace.

When they are all crying at once, let them. Take care of each child's needs one at a time. That's all you can do. Peace.

Although nothing is so important that you cannot interrupt it to dole out some attention, you should not always have to do so. Children need to know that the whole world is not going to stop for their every whim and that Mom's tasks are important, too. Sometimes you simply cannot stop everything, or perhaps the baby's needs must be met before you can shake a two-year-old off your leg.

Suggest, or give permission for, special activities. For example, let the children jump on the bed. (Gasp!) It is a treat for them and rattles loose some of that excess energy that is driving you wild. We have bed-jumping rules. They are not to stand on their feet to jump. Jumping on their knees distributes the weight more evenly (I think) and gives them more control over where they will land.

When my mother-in-law had ten preschool grandchildren, she allowed bed-jumping when they came to visit. She remembered what a "no-no" jumping on the bed had been when she was a child and how she enjoyed doing it anyway.

For the grandkids, the rule was enacted that once a child reached kindergarten, bed-jumping days at Grandma's were over. However, these children grew to be such

33

large boys and girls that a weight limit of forty pounds was also set. Most of those ten are now junior-high-school age, six feet tall and over, including a beautiful six-foot fourteen-year-old named Christine. I'm sure they all remember that Grandma let them jump on her bed and what fun they had doing it.

If feasible, suggest that they play outside. Kay says that no matter what the weather, her kids can always play outside. Kay lives in the country and need not worry about the street, the neighbor kids, the dogs, and so on. Sending little ones out when you need a break is not always a good idea, unless you can see them from your kitchen window or your resting chair.

Don't depend on mothers of the neighbor kids to supervise your tots unless you have a specific agreement. It is unfair to put another neighborhood mom in the position of being unofficial baby-sitter for the toddler set. Be responsible for your own kids and, of course, for the neighbor kids in your yard. It really is a special ministry.

By the way, never oil a squeaky tricycle. It's the best way I have of knowing exactly where my children are.

Use television without guilt. (Gasp, again!) Of course, I'm not suggesting that you plop a child down in front of "The Young and the Restless" day after day (or "The Young and the Rest of Us," as Bruce so profoundly calls it). But I have found that I can sometimes say, "Why don't you watch a little TV?" and we all feel better. That gives me the time I need to complete a task or catch my breath and then give them the attention they deserve. I prefer a little guilt-ridden TV to a lot of guilt-laden yelling.

Analyze what is causing your bad day. Debbi says anger is usually at the base of hers. She sometimes goes into her room and screams into a pillow for a few minutes.

Kathy gives credit for bad days to the child who doesn't get enough sleep, the weather, and too much sugar in the diet. She also says, "The more you talk about stress, the more you get." Kathy, you are absolutely right. As Kay says, "I keep hearing mothers say how busy they are. I just want to say 'Quit moaning about it.'"

There is a time to confess: "You know, I'm really having a tough time with all the responsibilities. Sometimes I think I'll go stark raving mad!" But I know that the more I think and the more I verbalize the idea that "Hey, we're doing okay here—I can handle it," the more I find that sure enough, we are doing fine.

Frustration is usually at the root of my bad days. I have a *Better Homes and Gardens* image of how my house should look, a *Glamour* magazine picture of how I should look, and a Norman Rockwell *Saturday Evening Post* cover idea of the perfect family. My list of things to do reads like this:

Clean bathroom

Bake cookies for church fellowship

Clean out boys' closets

Make Easter dress

Address Christmas cards

Write the great American novel

Find cure for cancer

A little unreasonable, huh? So are my expectations for myself sometimes. When I can't live up to them, my self-esteem takes a nose dive. When my self-confidence is out-to-lunch, so is my patience.

Expecting too much of young children always leads to tension. We forget that they are smaller and slower and so easily distracted by soaking up things about them. They also don't have to be anywhere on time.

Help them keep calm by not fretting over the soiled training pants, the shoe that keeps coming untied, the spilled juice, the dawdling over breakfast. Nancy says, "Don't sweat the little things." Roll with the punches. And get those children shoes with Velcro fastenings!

Don't set yourself up for situations that will make you crazy. If you don't want to walk into the kitchen and find every piece of bakeware you own on the floor, make the cabinet doors child-proof. Slip a yardstick through the handles or wind rubber bands around knobs that are next to each other. There are latches available for keeping the clamps on kitchen cabinets.

If you don't want the kids to eat your breath mints or drop your coins down the furnace register, keep your purse in a high place. I could use two refrigerators—the top of ours is piled so high with items to be kept out of the kids' reach.

If you don't want the baby to slobber all over your only clean outfit—the one you happen to be wearing—cover it up. I have a hand-me-down shirt that used to belong to my husband's huge-sized nephew and makes a perfect smock to wear while trying to get the rest of the family fed and dressed.

Know your limits. I cannot bake a double batch of cookies and fix a special-type meal in the same afternoon. It ruins me for the rest of the day.

Perhaps one of the biggest culprits of a bad day is our own physical exhaustion (reread chapter 2). When I'm well rested, I can handle almost anything. But you and I know firsthand what too little sleep can produce—fatigue, irritability, dizziness, sluggishness, indecision, and depression.

My sister-in-law told me of a friend of hers: "She just had her fourth baby, and she's only been married five years. She told her gynecologist that she's grouchy, cries a lot, and can't shake the depression. Her gynecologist sent her to a psychiatrist. My friend says, 'Well, I think it's helping some.'"

Though no expert, I think I recognize those symptoms. This gal is probably not eating enough of the foods that will sustain her and build her up, and with four children under five, she couldn't possibly be getting enough sleep.

Sleepy mother, do I have a Bible verse for you! "It is in vain that you rise up early and go late to rest, eating the bread of anxious toil; for he gives to his beloved sleep" (Ps. 127:2). *The Living Bible* says that last part, "God wants his loved ones to get their proper rest." Hallelujah!

If there is not an available grandma nearby, I would recommend that this gal hire a high-school girl to come in for an hour or two after school and keep the kids away from her so she can get her proper rest. (If problems seem to continue, professional help may be in order.)

All the baby books say, "Nap when the baby naps." They never say what to do with the other children while you and the baby are snoozing away. One mother enjoyed playing Cowboys and Indians with her children when they were little. Being "dead" gave her a chance to lie down with her eyes closed, if only for a few minutes.

Okay, the baby is asleep. Now to get those older children down for a nap. If they resist "nap time," call it "rest time." Let them sleep in a different bed from their own, or in a sleeping bag. Put on a calming record. Some adults fall asleep to a recording of ocean waves. Maybe your children would find certain music to be soothing and nap-conducive.

Tell them that they must lie on the bed until the oven timer goes off. Tell them that if they don't go to sleep before the big hand on the clock gets to, say, six, they can get up. Watching the clock will usually hypnotize them into slumber.

Put some cologne on their hands and tell them to smell it until all the scent is gone—ah! Deep breathing, restful sleep. Give back rubs. And rock. And rock. I've had to literally wrestle down an overly tired child in a rocking chair. But wrestling is okay. It wears them down.

If you cannot nap during the day, at least let the housework go and do something restful and relaxing. Call a friend, read a magazine, swish around alone in their wading pool, eat a pan of cinnamon rolls. Got the idea?

Help yourself back to life by splashing cold water on your face. Exercising a bit will get the oxygen pumped into your brain. A bit of bend-and-stretch at the kitchen sink can work wonders. Catch a tiny nap while rocking a child. At our house the rock-er usually falls asleep before the rock-ee.

I must admit, my worst time is night. During the day, when the boys' rowdiness with each other gets to be too much for me, I separate them from each other. At bedtime I separate them from me. That usually takes a great deal of energy, and I don't have much left over after the events of the day.

We have no trouble getting them into their pajamas. Don brought home T-shirts from a basketball tournament he played in. His team took second place. "I'm not about to wear a shirt that says 'Men's Senior League Second Place,'" he said, so they became ankle-length night shirts for Bruce and Roger. The boys have had them for many months now, and they still enjoy wearing them as if they were brand-new. When those are in the wash, they wear a different T-shirt belonging to Mommy or Daddy.

But ripping them away from roughhousing is a real fight. An oven timer is a handy device. "Okay, guys, you can have until the bell rings to play [ten minutes is good], then it's upstairs," or to the bathroom, or to the kitchen for snacks.

Kay, mother of three under four, says, "Don't get started with elaborate bedtime rituals." Before their third child was born, she would put her boys to bed with a song on the guitar. Then they would make up songs about things that happened during the day. They prayed for each individual cow, chicken, and pig on their farm. "Now," she says, "we just thank God for the animals. Amen."

I live with a little guilt at not being able to carry through the tuck-in-with-a-bedtime-story-list-of-who-loves-you-theologically-meaningful-prayer routine that I had envisioned as part of children's bedtime. Our kids' night-time personalities don't allow such a cozy scene. We do manage a prayer and lingering good-nights and I-love-you's. But the part about talking over the day and discussing all the wonderful things that are going to happen tomorrow usually has to be done well before bedtime.

No matter how distraught you are from trying to get the troops to bed—and I may be all wrong, for this may be a wonderful time for you at your house—calm down before saying good-night. That last bit is a loose translation of "... do not let the sun go down on your anger" (Eph. 4:26).

You may need to plop them in bed and say, "I'll be back in just a little bit to say good-night." Go into another room, catch your breath, pray for strength, then return with an improved bedside manner. Say the prayers, rub backs, do some deep breathing and sighing, think of pleasant things.

And then—the house is so quiet. I check the baby. Sweet baby. "Thank you, God, for this dear little child. I still can hardly believe he is ours."

I go upstairs to see that the boys are warm enough. I probably had opened up the windows too wide—we worked up such a sweat trying to get them to bed and out of each other's way. They have fallen asleep. They were so tired. Growing up is such hard work.

Thank you, Jesus. Already I'm looking forward to hearing their little voices in the morning.

5

Two Tools of the Trade

Two Tools of the Trade

Discipline is one of the best tools for peace. Kathy M., who raised five lovely daughters, says, "Above all, be firm. Say what you mean and be able to follow through on what you say. If you have well-disciplined kids, you simply won't have some of the problems that make coping a difficulty."

The Bible tells us that children need strict, consistent discipline in order to develop strength of character. The purpose of discipline is not to punish and not to let you vent your anger. "Be angry, but do not sin . . ." (Eph. 4:26). Along with developing character, the purpose of discipline is to teach. One thing a child must learn is that there are direct consequences of his or her actions.

We use a little device at our house that has avoided many knock-down-drag-outs. I call it the "one-two-three ultimatum," but many parents use this little magic trick. After presenting a *reasonable* and *specific* request to a child one or more times in a nonthreatening manner without getting results, simply state, "If you don't get over here in front of me by the time I count to three [or whatever seems reasonable], I will spank."

Do not count, "One, two, two and a half, two and three-fourths. . . ." The formula is: one, pause, two, pause, three, spank. You'd be amazed at how early in life a child can relate to this ultimatum. Even our strong-willed Roger meets our request before the count of three.

One mother of three preschoolers uses "now" as her ultimatum word. She first calmly makes the request with "please." If she gets no action, she makes the request firmer and without "please." No action yet? She then makes the request again, using the magic word *NOW!* Those kids scramble!

Some parents do not advocate a warning system before spanking. A young child, though, is so distracted that he or she really needs a "break." Of course, the situation will dictate this need. As our oldest child matures, we don't give him the one-two-three business as often as we did when he was younger. He should have the message by now that we mean what we say.

To get a child to stop doing something or to reinforce a warning, just say, "If you throw that, I will spank." "If you touch that knob, I will spank." "If you grab that away from your brother, I will spank." *Then do it!* Without guilt.

Carol says, "Maybe I should feel guilty. When I spank him, it doesn't hurt me more than it hurts him." Of course not. You are exercising your parental authority.

It is important to have a verbal control device. Since your arms are often full of baby, you cannot possibly always physically maneuver the older child into doing as told. You may need to put the baby down a few times and let him cry while you administer the promised spanking, but the results will be worth the inconvenience.

A spanking, now, is not a "whippin'." Remember, "Be angry, but do not sin." A spanking is a sharp swat on the rear end for the purpose of getting the offender's attention and for letting a child know who is boss. To be effective, and to have any meaning, spank immediately after the offense. For toddlers, this "wait until your father gets home" stuff doesn't work. Their memories are not sufficiently developed enough to understand that this

43

is justice—and it's not fair to make Daddy the perpetual heavy.

There are alternatives to spanking that may be just as effective, depending on the child. There can be a "time out." This is a sit-in-the-corner-until-the-oven-timer-rings. Five minutes is enough. Send the child to his or her room, or take away a privilege. Remember, though, that punishment needs to be immediate. Also, what works for one of your children may not work for another.

Save yelling only for the "biggies." The more you yell, the less they'll listen. Memorize this verse: "She opens her mouth with wisdom, and the teaching of kindness is on her tongue" (Prov. 31:26).

Don't be shocked the first time you hear "I hate you!" or "You're the worst mommy in the whole world!" Andrea's neighbor called her in tears the first time her three-year-old uttered these immortal phrases. Her self-esteem was so low that she did not understand that that's the way kids are. Instead she took it personally, not realizing that in ten minutes her daughter would be in an entirely different frame of mind. You are not the camp counselor. You are the mom.

Important: after a session of crime and punishment, after the tears are over, tell your child how much you love him or her and talk about why the punishment occurred. The child will experience the security of knowing someone is setting limits and will realize that this person is still a loving parent.

My dad is six-foot-four. When he speaks, people listen. As children we always knew we were being punished, why it occurred, and that we'd better not let it happen again. I remember some spankings and I remember scoldings. Always, after the scoldings, when we felt ashamed at what we had or had not done, Dad made a joke, helped us laugh. Oh, how it quelled the fires of embarrassment over our misdeeds and made us certain that we were still very much loved. Children want to please their parents (authority figures) and know they are loved.

I really believe you should tell a child the why's of both the request and the punishment. "Because I said so" should be used sparingly. However, there are times when you can simply assert your authority with "because I said so." Isn't that the way it is with God? We want to ask, "Why?" Often the answer is "because I am God"—God, the great "I am."

As a child gets older, spankings can be less frequent, and other means of punishment can be used. Bruce started school this year. Along with school worksheets and proclamations of love for his teacher, he brought home words that are not even used on television. We reasoned with him over the rudeness of those words and insisted that there are more intelligent ways of expressing oneself. Okay, fine. Then we got the report from the neighbor kids that Bruce was calling them a you-know-what. (If you don't know "what," I won't repeat it.) Bruce got grounded. He did it again. He got grounded for two days in a row—no neighbor kids over, no visiting the neighbors, no friends after school. We haven't heard such words since.

There are times when doing nothing is the best course of action. Twice, Bruce sprinkled baby powder all over our bedroom. Each time, I yelled, spanked, and warned what would happen if he did it again. (Like a dummy, I also put the powder back within reach each time.) The third time it happened, there was nothing I could do. I was too angry and had seen the lack of results with previous methods. I calmly got out the vacuum cleaner and helped him clean up the mess. It never happened again.

Another time, Bruce was waiting for Don in our old work truck. They were going to take a load of brush out to the dump. I was inside the house giving a piano lesson. Suddenly the door opened and in walked Bruce with the strangest look on his face. I asked, "Aren't you going to the dump with Daddy?" He stood silently at the door, then ran into the baby's room and "hid" under the crib. He had knocked the gearshift into neutral, and the truck had rolled backward out of the driveway and hit the car parked across the street. The teenage owner of the car was extremely unhappy. We were thankful nothing more serious happened. Bruce was plain petrified. A policeman came to take an accident report, and the next day in our newspaper the whole thing was written up in the police blotter. By the look of terror on his face, we knew Bruce had already taken the consequences. We chose to downplay the incident completely, mention it only when he wasn't around, and quietly cut out the clipping for his baby book.

Being firm with the children while they are very young not only gives you the control that you need, but it sets limits for them that they so desperately need and want. If you are firm with them now, you can always ease up later. It's like the painful lesson I learned my first year of teaching—don't smile until Thanksgiving. Once they are school age it is very difficult to get useful results from discipline if you only then suddenly decide it's time for you to take control.

The best advice ever given to me about getting along with a youngster came after months of frustration with two-year-old Roger. "Oh! I just can't control that boy!" I wailed to my mother.

Immediately she replied, "Don't let him know that."

Wow! That was the beginning of a new day for Roger and me.

In practical, working terms, what she said was, "You should know by now to expect the crying and whining jags. As long as you know you are doing your best to meet his needs and comfort his moods, you do not have to take his fussiness and demands so seriously. Just roll with his punches."

Amazing! As my attitude toward Roger's behavior has changed, so has he. He's still moody and fussy, but that seems to be part of being Roger. What can you say about a two-year-old whose favorite snack is hot Mexican picante sauce? Now that I recognize his message, "Love me, love my moods," I'm finding so much more to enjoy about that boy.

Using praise is right up there with using discipline to keep the peace. Praise will help head off those situations that call for parental exercise of authority. Praise means "catching" the child doing as you wish and praising him for it. "Thank you for being such a good boy at the table." "Thank you for sharing with your brother." "I'm so proud of the way you picked up your toys the first time I asked you."

Redbook magazine published an article by Donna Lawson on praise. I'd like to pass along the main points.

1. No matter how much you give, you can always give more. A child's behavior is linked to his self-esteem. Praise encourages good behavior and good self-esteem.

2. Be specific, immediate, and don't qualify. Tell the child what action or deed he is "terrific" for, or he'll not know what he is capable of doing. Just as immediate discipline is important, so is immediate praise, in order for it to be effective. Don't say, "You did good, but...."

3. You have to really mean it. "Otherwise, you'll shape your child's behavior but not his character . . . you'll get a youngster who is performance oriented."

4. Above all, empathize. Try to sense what the child needs at the moment.

5. Say yes instead of no. Show your child he has your attention before he misbehaves in an attempt to get it.

6. Don't equate your child's worthiness with what he does or doesn't do. "Never say, 'I love you for cleaning your room,' but rather, 'You did a good job cleaning your room.'" Similarly, don't say, "You're a bad boy," but rather, "I don't like what you're doing."

7. Encourage reasonable risk-taking. Be there for them and to cheer them on when they pick themselves up and try again. A sense of self-worth goes a long way in resisting peer pressure when they are older. (And let me tell you, it won't be long. We've had some incredible incidents in kindergarten.) It is risky not to go along with the crowd. But it is a risk that the parents can make a child feel proud for taking.

8. Use praise to help your child finish tasks. Nudge him with the good job he's done so far and how terrific it will be when it's finished.

9. Coordinate your praise with what the child gets at school. Have good communication with others who are helping train your child (preschool teacher, Sunday-school teacher, nursery worker).

10. Praise must flow from Dad as well as Mom. "Daddy and I are proud . . ." makes it twice as nice.[1]

Tony Campolo, in *It's Friday, But Sunday's Comin'*, tells of growing up as a member of an Italian minority in a Jewish and black neighborhood. He says the Jewish kids amazed him—they were so successful and self-confident. (They produce more Nobel Prize winners per capita than any other ethnic group.) Campolo attributes the success of Jewish kids and adults to their mothers: "Their culture has built into motherhood the idea that the primary responsibility of a mother is to build up her child and make the child feel special. Consequently, Jewish kids grow up thinking that they are wonderful."[2]

If the child flunks first grade, the typical "Jewish mother" response is "It just goes to show—they don't know how to educate a genius down there at that school."[3]

Self-esteem is one of the most important things parents can give their children. Self-esteem is a comforting lap when they have outgrown yours.

Remember Romans 14:19? "Let us then pursue what makes for peace and for mutual upbuilding." And 1 Thessalonians 5:11 says, "Therefore encourage one another and build one another up. . . ."

Issuing praise and encouragement will not only help keep these early years peaceful, but it will give your children the confidence they need in order to face the world. Encourage!

Notes

1. Donna Lawson, "Applause! Applause! How to Handle Your Kids With Praise," *Redbook*, June 1984, pp. 86–87, 156.

2. Anthony Campolo, *It's Friday, But Sunday's Comin'* (Waco, Texas: Word Books, 1984), p. 29.

3. *Ibid.*, p. 29.

6

When I Say No I Feel
(a) Guilty
(b) Wonderful
(c) All of the Above

When I Say No I Feel
(a) Guilty
(b) Wonderful
(c) All of the Above

My husband uses the direct approach in dealing with me. "You know," he said one day as I was packing up the diaper bag, "if you're going to be a stay-at-home mother, you really ought to stay at home."

Well, no wonder I didn't miss my job as much as I thought I would. I was on too many shopping errands, attending too many meetings, and burning too much gasoline to justify calling myself a real stay-at-home mom.

If you have several preschoolers, you are probably in that category. And let's face it, the world needs stay-at-home moms. Every church committee, women's group, and PTA needs you. Every fund-raising drive and not-for-profit organization wants you. Your name is probably on the nominating committee's list for every group you have ever been associated with. But, Mom, your family needs you first.

Joy says that every time she unloads home-baked goodies from the oven, her husband says, "Who are those for this time?"

And when Donna's husband says, "Okay, you can go to that meeting, but only if you learn something," he is really saying, "Don't forget that your first responsibility is to take care of your family. We need you."

"No" is one of the first words our children learn. But as women who have been taught that we have responsibility to others of the world, it is one of the last words we learn to use.

People who ask you if you would be on this committee or that either never knew, or have forgotten, what life with little ones is like. They assure you that you can do the job, and you may know that you can. Before you know it, you have one more time-consuming responsibility, one more search for a baby-sitter, one more load and unload the kids from the car, one more time to wake the baby from a nap so you can get to your meeting.

Saying no takes practice. Saying no without guilt takes conviction. My husband and I were recently asked to become members of a worthwhile and honorable group. So worthwhile, in fact, that the recruiter handed out application forms with the announcement that we would not even need to pray about this because "God wants you here."

While it was an honor to be asked to join, I didn't appreciate this fellow's approach. I had already prayed about it—months before we were asked.

If I get involved in one more noble cause or worthy organization, my children will lament from their jail cells years from now, "My mother was never home." My husband says I'm exaggerating, but you get the point.

There will always be worthwhile causes, but not always a two-year-old in your lap. There will always be committee meetings you can attend, but not always a baby to rock and cuddle. There will always be a fund-raising drive, but not always a preschooler who wants you to read to him. Your family does not deserve only your leftover time. They deserve your best time.

I am learning to take Thoreau's advice—one brief word, three times over—"Simplify! Simplify! Simplify!" If this extra demand will cause complications in an already hectic life, I can say no. My family's happiness is at stake.

If it means attending meetings with no baby-sitting provided, I can say no. My family's budget is at stake.

If it means boxes of material and literature, pamphlets, and notebooks that would take up space where the playpen should be, I can say no. My family's home base is threatened.

If it means a truly nerve-wracking experience and one for which I am ill-prepared, I can say no. For example, my disastrous experience of teaching three-year-olds at Bible school. My emotional well-being is at stake, and if that is, so is my family's peace.

If it means that when I hang up the phone after saying no, I feel relieved that I haven't added another burden to my family, I am assured that "no" was the right answer.

How do you say no?

You can say, "I really need to talk this over with my husband." More than once, Don has put the word *no* into my mouth, and I have been so grateful he has. It's okay for me to use him as an excuse. He understands better than I do that what I take on involves the whole family, just by virtue of the time I must spend in order to do a good job.

You can say what Donna said when she was asked to serve on a church board: "Ask me again in five years, when all my kids are in school. Then I will be happy to do anything."

You can say, "Thank you very much for asking me. I'm pleased that you think I can do the job, but right now my family responsibilities come first." You are not using your family as an excuse, but as a reason.

Don't tell the person doing the asking that you are "too busy." That person is also busy and will probably tell you so. You will wind up feeling guilty and maybe saying yes to something you really can't give proper attention.

I am not, of course, suggesting that you drop out of sight altogether. There are other ways of saying no. If you really can't teach Bible school this year, volunteer to bake cookies or play the piano for opening exercises. If you can't help serve a funeral dinner, volunteer to baby-sit another mother's child while she helps.

One mother of three expressed frustration at not being able to get out and around like she used to, so that she could participate in service activities and go visiting. She need not worry too much. This gal answers her phone every time it rings with "Hello, Jesus loves you." She has caught more than a few telephone solicitors off guard, but she performs a service nonetheless.

Welcoming the neighbor kids to play in your yard is service, as is sending cards to the sick and shut-ins. So is sending thank-you notes to faithful church workers. Calling a friend to offer encouragement, support, and prayer is service. Call or drop a card to a visitor who came to your Sunday-school class or church service. The newcomer will return. That's service.

You can clip newspaper articles and birth announcements to send to acquaintances whose names are mentioned in the paper. You can cut quilt blocks, take in mending from the white-cross box, write to missionaries, or offer to address envelopes for church mailings—if your church has no secretary and your pastor can get them over to you. There are many ways to serve others from your home. Pray for guidance in finding creative means of service if you feel housebound and not of much use to the world's "others."

And don't forget that those famous "others" whom we are called upon to serve also include our children. One mother of six, whose oldest child was eight years old, felt that she could never be of use to the Lord as long as all she could do was take care of her children's needs. Her mother-in-law set her straight: "If you raise these children for the Lord and so that they want to live for him, you have done a missionary's job."

Whether you have one child or one dozen, the mission field is right under your roof—probably at your elbow right now, asking for a cookie. Simplify your life so that you can really concentrate on those who need you at home base.

Mom, if you're tempted to work a full-time job outside the home, let me give you one person's story—which just happens to be mine.

I never expected to be a stay-at-home mom. Back that up a few years. I never really considered getting married and having a family. But praise the Lord, it happened. God's plan for me was much more exciting than my plans for myself.

Don and I never even talked about the possibility that I would not hold a job. Even if we had not needed my income to supplement his salary as a teacher and coach, I did not consider that there would ever be a time my job description would be "homemaker."

I taught high-school English. Between teaching jobs, I had other employment. I worked in public relations for a book and magazine distributing company; I worked for a government social-service agency; and for a time I was an almost full-time substitute teacher.

Teaching was my love, my reputation, my identity. I was proud to say I was a teacher, happy to be introduced as a teacher. I was pleased to work with other professionals in a stimulating environment, and I even liked the students.

I was eight months pregnant with Roger, our second son, and in the last few weeks before my maternity leave from school, which would begin with Thanksgiving vacation. Don had recently been to a regional church convention and had not said much about it—until now.

"You know," he said, "the speakers talked a lot about getting back to basics. I think we should consider the possibility of your not working."

All I could do was cry—not because I did not want to leave my job, but because I could not believe what I was hearing. I knew at once there was nothing to consider. I would resign my beloved job at the end of the school year. I could hardly wait.

It was a risk for Don to "allow me" to quit working. We enjoyed the money and thought we needed it. But we knew we could trust the Lord financially. We had seen him meet our needs so many times before and were ready to take this step of faith.

But what about my personal needs? What about the pride I had in holding that job, all the things about working that I enjoyed? When I gave those concerns to the Lord, he took care of my desire to have an identity with a profession. In my role as a mom I have not lost who I am. I don't even mind being called a housewife. I know the Lord had to have a hand in that!

Several months ago I opened the front door to a new Avon representative in my area. As we chatted, I learned that she has three little boys not much older than my three. She also goes to school full-time and now had taken up this part-time job. She explained, "Oh, I'm not one of those women who can sit around at home all day doing nothing." Nothing! You've got to be kidding!

I have heard many women say that staying at home is boring. I can't help thinking that being bored is their own fault. Sure, the at-home routine can be frustrating but it doesn't need to be boring. I felt sorry for this woman. And I felt sorry for her family. I would have liked to encourage her to give it a chance, but she quickly changed the subject when she realized that she might be talking to "one of those women."

If you have a job outside the home, are thinking about getting one, or think you're just "not the type" to stay at home with children, trust the Lord to meet your psychological needs as well as your financial ones.

Our home is much more relaxed since I quit my job. Before, all of our family time was consumed by getting bottles and diaper bags ready for the next day. In the morning we were out the door by seven-thirty. This business about spending "quality" rather than "quantity" time with the children sounds good, but it just doesn't work.

Marilee Horton, in *Free to Stay at Home*, suggests asking yourself these questions:

1. Why am I working?
2. What would happen if I didn't work?
3. How would the family suffer if I stopped working?
4. How would the family benefit if I were to be a full-time keeper of the home?[1]

Sure, those questions may seem a little irrelevant to you as the dryer buzzes and you trot off to throw in another load of diapers. But at a time when a diminishing number of women understand that it takes guts to stay at home, it doesn't hurt to think about your own job description. (It is certainly not my purpose to offend working mothers. I just want to give some support to those who don't pull in a paycheck.)

My husband has become a strong advocate of stay-at-home motherhood. He encourages men at school who have young children and working wives to think about affirming a mom's right to stay at home. He enthusiastically supports couples in their decision to have the woman stay home. He tells the men that sure, some financial sacrifices may need to be made, or that they may need to put in extra hours at a part-time job, but that it's worth it.

If you are a stay-at-home mom, be proud that you are. Don't apologize for letting God's plan for mothers be at work in your life. Relish your position as a rebel in a secular society. Use your position to God's honor and glory.

Note

1. Marilee Horton, *Free to Stay at Home* (Waco, Texas: Word Books, 1982), p. 66.

7

Give Me a Break

Give Me a Break

Maybe your phone is not ringing off the wall with offers to belong to this group or that, or to take an office in some worthwhile organization. Maybe you think that just because no one has asked you to do something, no one wants you to. Maybe the thought of leaving the house after being cooped up so many days with the children gives you a rash. Maybe you think it's not worth the hassle of loading the kids into the car.

Mom, you've got to get out of that house. You have to talk to someone over three feet tall. You need a break, and frankly, so do your kids.

Start saying yes to the outside world.

One Sunday after church, Gloria's husband took the pastor's wife aside to thank her for what Gloria's involvement with church activities had done for their marriage and home life: "She feels useful outside of our home and is excited about the things going on around her."

Now don't rush right out and sign up to teach Sunday school, be president of the women's group, sing in the choir, type church bulletins, and head up the Christmas pageant. But do look into what your church has to offer. Try the women's groups. You'll get lots of support from the younger women and plenty of sympathy from the older ones. Involvement in a mission circle is a good place to start.

In addition to circle groups, our church has a twice-a-month study group called Mothers and Others. It's for those of us who need it most. We have a program, Bible study, lots of socializing, and bountiful sharing.

I keep thinking, "Oh, so-and-so could be getting so much out of this group," or, "I really miss having so-and-so here. She has such good ideas." Although I invite, offer rides, make announcements in Sunday-school classes, there are just some moms afraid to take that first step outside of the church pew they keep warm on Sunday morning. If you are one of those people, please reconsider. Don't deprive other mothers of your support or yourself of their fellowship.

The key to being able to attend get-togethers at the church is "nursery provided." I am fortunate to belong to a church where a nursery is available during every meeting. It is considered part of the ministry of the church and is an annual budgeted item.

Dear Grandma Blake, as she is known to the hundreds who have passed through the Dutch doors of her nursery, has been at it for forty-eight years. She lovingly tends babies of babies she knew years ago. ("He looks just like his daddy when he was a baby.") Now in her seventies, Grandma Blake can still bend down to pick up a tumbled toddler and remember which diaper bag belongs to what baby. She is our church's treasure.

If your church does not provide a nursery during meetings that mothers of young children are likely to attend, perhaps it is because no one has asked. Talk with your pastor. Offer to help search for just the right individual—perhaps a grandmother or retired lady. College students are available at certain times of the day, or there may be a young mother who needs the money. (We pay our church sitters minimum wage.)

It remains the church's business, once it has set up a

61

program for adults, to see that they are encouraged to come. "Nursery provided" is one of those ways.

I tend to be a little hesitant to be involved in activities outside of church. For one thing, I have to find and pay for my own sitter. If I need a sitter in the evenings, I start at the top of the list of high-school girls our boys enjoy having around and telephone until I find one. Finding the money to pay is sometimes a problem. But as Judy, mother of four, says, "You can't afford not to go out."

When Alex was tiny, I was reluctant to leave one sitter in charge of all three boys. So I hired two sitters if we went out in the evenings—friends or sisters. Finally one of them said, "Look, I can handle it alone." Every sitter assures me that she has had no problems the whole evening. One of these times I'm going to hide behind the drapes to see how she does it. Kids enjoy having a new face in the house, even if you can hear them crying all the way out to the car.

As for child-care during the day, Kay says, "Live in the same town with lots of relatives and never make your mother mad." Oh, I envy my friends whose kids have a grandparent in town. They are, of course, sensitive about child-care arrangements with Grandma. Grandmothers these days are not at home baking chocolate-chip cookies for their little darlin's. They are nurses, teachers, bookkeepers, secretaries, artists, choir directors, and club presidents. Remember, this is the time in Grandma's life when she is doing those things she put "on hold" while her children were young.

A baby-sitting co-op is a child-care solution for many mothers. One group in our town works on a point system. Members earn points by baby-sitting; they spend points by using a sitter. The more children in a family, the more points earned or spent. Time is also figured in points.

A meeting is held every three months, and chairperson responsibilities are changed at that time. The job of secretary rotates each month. A person wanting a sitter calls the secretary, who calls members until she finds a sitter available. The secretary also has the list of work phone numbers, doctors' names, and allergies and medical conditions of the children.

The sitter whom the secretary has found then calls the person needing child-care to tell her she can do it. After the "sit," the sitter reports her points earned to the secretary.

There are also provisos regarding the time spent in sitting, safety guidelines, and membership rules. The nice things about a co-op are that no money is exchanged, a mother knows she will always be able to have someone sit, and the sitters are known to be reliable.

Of course, there is the more informal arrangement of calling up a friend and asking, "Can you keep the kids for an hour or so this morning?" Unless I'm going to a doctor, shopping in a china shop, or paying by the hour, I try to take at least one child with me. I just feel that three children under five is a bit of an imposition on a mother who is not related to me. Besides, I enjoy sharing some special time with one boy at a time.

Another reason I am reluctant to get involved in activities outside my church is that I am so comfortable with my Christian friends. Now that I'm not working, I really don't have very much contact with non-Christians. I love my sheltered life of church friends and fellowship with Christian mothers. But, as our pastor says, all the church meetings and do-good activities are merely digging for worms—not fishing for men. I need to exercise my Christianity by taking it outside the Christian community. If you feel this way, or just want other ways to get out of the house occasionally, here are some suggestions:

Take a craft class—you'll meet other women while learning a new technique or sharpening a skill.

Take an exercise class—money well spent.

Join a hobby club. I go to a quilt guild; Don goes to computer club on the same night—money well spent on a sitter.

Join a diet group. If you need to lose weight, this group will help you do so healthfully. Do not put your family through the pain of your crash diet.

Watch the calendar section of your local newspaper for a group that interests you.

Have a home sales party, inviting a sprinkling of women who don't go to church with you.

You don't have to be involved in an organized group or activity to give yourself the break you deserve. One mother took her very young sons to a day-care program one day a week. The budget was tight, but her husband recognized this as an important item.

Arrange with a friend for trade or pay to take the kids for one or two mornings a week on a regular basis. Do errands, have coffee with a neighbor, go to the library and read their magazines, take a nap, go out for donuts with a friend, keep a journal, write a book. . . .

Don't feel guilty about taking a break. Doesn't your husband ever fall asleep in an easy chair or just sit in front of the TV after work? He's taking a break. Since you're on duty twenty-four hours a day, you deserve a break, too.

Don had gone to a meeting one evening. I had spent a horrendous time getting the kids to bed and had just sprawled out on the couch with a bowl of popcorn to stare zombie-eyed at a prime-time soap opera. In walked Don. I quickly regrouped myself and explained that I had been working most of the evening. You know, he got really upset that I would feel I had to explain why I was just lying around. I should give him more credit for being understanding about my responsibilities.

Unless you are having a sitter come in or your husband is home with the children, getting out of the house means packing up the kids. It is not easy to get more than one little one from Point A to Point B.

Plan ahead. Pack the diaper bag the night before. Have a bottle of formula or milk in the fridge. Even though I breast-fed each baby, I always took along formula when going places. On days we stayed at home, I gave one bottle of formula—or Daddy did. He should share some of the joys of grocery duty.

If the children are going to a sitter, be considerate in what you pack in the diaper bag. Include some Wet Wipes (make your own with damp paper towels stored in a plastic container) so the sitter won't have to use her own washcloths for the baby's dirty bottom. Also send a rubberized pad to put the baby on when changing, extra diaper pins, and spare pants for your supposedly toilet-trained toddler.

Think of your car as a giant diaper bag. Pack extra clothes for all; keep crackers or dry cereal in an airtight container. One change of clothes may suffice for two youngsters if they are near the same size. Hopefully, they won't both need an emergency change at the same time.

Keep the kids' jackets, hats, and gloves in one place. Ours are stationed alongside the front door. At child level is a board with three pegs for hanging coats and jackets. It was purchased very cheaply at a discount store in the bathroom-fixtures department. I was even able to install it myself. In the closet keep a basket hanging on a string at child level—one for gloves and mittens, one for hats.

I also have a hanging basket for keys at Mommy level. As I walk in the door, I toss in my keys. They are always there when I'm next ready for them. Tie a brightly colored piece of cloth or yarn pompom to your key ring. If the keys do get misplaced, they are so much easier to find, and the children can help you track them down if they are looking for something that will catch their eye. Always remember to look under and between the couch cushions!

Try to enforce a parking place for shoes. More than

once, I have carried a shoeless child out to the car when his shoes just didn't turn up and we were already tardy.

Load the baby into a canvas carrier. Be careful about what kind you purchase. Some of them take a degree in engineering to maneuver the baby into.

And now aim for the car seats. Strap in young children securely. Never, never hold a child on your lap or let him stand in the seat, even if you are just backing out of the driveway. Position older children in seat belts and harnesses at opposite doors to avoid All Star wrestling in the car.

Upon destination—let's say, the church parking lot—unload Baby, put the sling of the baby carrier around your neck, and start searching for someone else getting out of her car to help you grab the diaper bag and the other children.

No luck? Swing the diaper bag over your shoulder or come back later for it, and let the other children loose from their seat belts. Make them get out on the same side of the car as you and stick beside it like glue until you give marching orders. Use your free hand to grasp the toddler's hand (don't pull off his mitten). Any older children know very well they had better stay by Mama. This parking-lot business can be dangerous stuff!

Kids safely deposited? Okay, Mom, go do your thing!

Expand your world and share it with your family. I always hate to see young women get married as soon as (or before) they graduate from high school. Getting out in the world by going to college or trade school, holding a job, traveling, or moving away from home gives a person much more to bring to a marriage.

Motherhood is like that, too. Expanding interests, giving to others, and partaking of activities that are going on outside the home give a woman so much more to bring to her family. You can talk with your husband about things other than how many times Junior made it to the potty chair today or how long the baby napped.

Life at home is exciting. Share that with other people. Life outside your home is also exciting. Share that with your family.

8

Come On In—If You Can Find a Path

Come On In—If You Can Find a Path

Don and I went to a Sunday-school-class party where we played an Oldywed version of the Newlywed Game. Sounds dangerous, doesn't it?

One particularly provocative question was: "Will your husband say you are, or are not, a good housekeeper?" That was easy for some. Brenda was a home-ec major in college. She had better be a good housekeeper. Donna B. is also good at housekeeping—she claims it's her "therapy."

Connie's house is a mess and she knows it. "If the beds are made, my husband thinks the house is clean. If I have slaved all day cleaning house but the beds are not made, he thinks the house is a mess. So I don't make beds. It's my point of rebellion." Hmm.

Nancy, who is an excellent housekeeper, says that her husband wishes she would not work so hard at it. About making beds, he says, "Why bother? They will just get unmade soon enough."

Men view things differently than women. Donna was so proud when she had just given the house a thorough going-over before unexpected company arrived. However, when her husband got home, he said, "Do you mean they saw the house like this?" He was referring to an unfinished sewing project left out in the utility room. Donna was crushed.

Several times I have told Don, "Well, I think I am doing

70

pretty good with the house, considering the age of the kids and all the projects I have going on." So I answered the game question with, "As good as can be expected at this point in my life."

And Don answered, "It's a good thing she can write." We were awarded the points.

As demonstrated by various responses to our version of the Newlywed Game, everyone has a different style of housekeeping. But if there are young children, two things are certain: (1) there will be clutter; and (2) there will be more clutter.

The goal is to live with clutter by organizing it. Don't let the clutter control you. Let me demonstrate. When we built our family room, I had the lovely philosophy that "this is the kids' room, too. After all, they're family. They should be allowed to keep some of their toys here."

Consequently there was a stream of toys spilling out of the upstairs toy box, making a river down the stairs, and emptying into the ocean of the family room. There were several tributaries in the living room, kitchen, and bathroom. At cleanup time it was impossible to know what should go upstairs and what could be kept in the family room. I was constantly complaining about toys scattered everywhere and literally had to forge a path from the kitchen to the bedroom.

My husband solved this problem one day while I was out shopping. "I put all of the toys upstairs, except for a few of Alex's," he announced. "If Bruce or Roger wants a toy, he brings it downstairs. At the end of the day, we won't have to make those awful decisions about what goes where. It all goes upstairs." Smart man. As a result we are much more relaxed in our family room and are no longer waking up to mountains of Lego pieces, Lincoln Logs, and Loc Blocks.

Many families go around at the end of the day with a plastic laundry basket, picking up the toys and depositing them in their rightful places. Some mothers threaten to throw away anything that the children haven't picked up when they've been asked to do so. My mother used to get out the dust mop and say, "Okay! I'm throwing away everything in my path!" We scrambled! Save that threat for when the kids are older and use it only if prepared to follow through. Some mothers hold scattered toys for ransom—pay a certain amount into the family kitty or do a certain nasty job, and the toy is returned. Again, this may be better strategy for older children.

Being able to deposit toys in their rightful places is the key to the kids' ability to help out. The best watchword of good housekeeping is still: "A place for everything and everything in its place."

I have heard, seen, and read that shelves are the best bet for turning Toyland into Joyland (a phrase borrowed from the book I mention below). The kids can see where the toys belong, making it easier both for putting them away and getting them out. It does no good to have a cigar box for little plastic firemen if it is buried at the bottom of the toy box. If the kids want to play with the firemen, they have to dump out everything on top. Chances are, they won't want to play with any toy they can't see. Debbi says that when her children had toy boxes, they never played with their toys. Out of sight, out of mind. Debbi's kids now have shelves.

The shelves can be anything from particle board and cinder blocks to the hand-stained and varnished variety. Here's how to organize those shelves, as described by Deniece Schofield in her book *Confessions of an Organized Housewife*. My friend Donna uses this system, as does our church nursery and day-care unit. It works.

Use plastic containers such as dishpans or empty ice-cream pails to store toy pieces. Label the containers with permanent marker, draw pictures, or use magazine cutouts for "Cowboys and Indians," "Fisher-Price people," "trains," "doll furniture," and so on. Use laundry baskets for large-size toys such as dump trucks and Care Bears.[1]

(Now take some of those toys and put them away in a closet where the kids will forget about them. In six months, bring them out and rotate. It will be like having new toys.)

Schofield says to forget about using the bookshelves for books. If books are standing neatly in a row with their pictureless spines showing, the child will have to pull out all the books to find the one he wants. Worse yet, he may bypass the books altogether. Dishpans, again, or new kitty-litter boxes are the answer. Stack the books with covers facing front, so that when your child wants a book, all he has to do is flip through the selections, file-style.[2]

For coloring books and crayons, get a plastic ice-cube bin to dump the crayons in. (We use a cigar box that we can put a rubber band around so Alex won't get into it and eat the crayons. An old covered lunch pail also works well.) Stash the coloring books in the dishpan behind the crayons. There are also on the market nifty divided bins with a carrying handle.[3]

Now tell your husband that you are going to spend his next hard-earned check on dishpans and kitty-litter boxes!

Eliminate the little aggravations. (No, no, I don't mean send the kids to the neighbor's!) Since our kids like to dress in the family room, their pajamas were never put away. Running upstairs to tuck away pajamas was not a top priority on anyone's list. They were usually left in a wad on the stairway or maneuvered their way between couch cushions. For less than a dollar, I bought a bright blue rack with six (count 'em) hooks and hung it in the stairwell at the foot of the stairs. The p.j.'s are always put away now. If they're dirty, the laundry room is two feet away.

Get hooked! Hang up anything you can. Dump toys with many pieces into bags with handles and hang them up.

Keep dress-up play clothes, fireman's hats, and Superman capes on hooks. An expandable accordion-type coat rack provides good storage for anything from coffee mugs and scarves to shoe bags and baseball gloves.

Nancy's five kids have such an abundance of stuffed toys that she hangs them on the walls of bedrooms. If not played with, they are at least seen and enjoyed.

The best thing about having a toy system is that the children know where things belong. If you are not encouraging them now to pick up and put away, you will spend their teenage years nagging at them. Don't give them an excuse to be slobs!

Mrs. Lowrey, who had five children in six years, says that if she could do it all over again, she would teach the kids to pick up their toys at the end of the day. Here's how to do it:

Announce that you're going to "blitz" the living room. Set the timer for five to seven minutes (any longer and they lose interest and enthusiasm), then help them see how much can be accomplished before the buzzer goes off. If before bedtime is too hectic or you are too tired then to be much of a forewoman, you may want to try this right after supper or even before Daddy gets home. Whenever you do it, get your kids into the habit of helping.

Aren't there more important things than keeping a clean house? You bet there are! I would be embarrassed if my house were clinically clean. It would mean that I am spending too much time turning mattresses and dusting picture frames and not enough time with my children. Verletta says, "I had everything in its place at the expense of the children. I was such a perfectionist. I needed to be more flexible."

But keeping *some* order is important. In her book *Handbook for Christian Homemakers*, Edith Flowers Kilgo says this about a place for everything:

Have you ever noticed how orderly are the things of God's creation? Everything God designed has its own place to be and, if not disturbed by mankind, God's handiwork remains organized and tidy. Polar bears don't try to live in Florida. The sun doesn't rise from the south instead of the east. Everything God has designed follows an orderly pattern and fulfills His purpose.

But it is not always that way in our homes. Sometimes it is difficult to find the things we want to find, and time is wasted in the search. Christians are expected to be good stewards of their time as well as their money.[4]

If you have a difficult time keeping up with things, or you just don't care, perhaps you are suffering from a lack of self-esteem. This is a letter that appeared recently in the Ann Landers newspaper column.

I was one of the most shameless slobs in the world and everyone knew it. One day, at age 27, I realized there must be a reason I was satisfied to live in a pigpen. I began to delve into my mind (couldn't afford a counselor) and discovered a clutter that took six years to tidy up. My problems ranged from being abused as a child to a total lack of self-esteem.

The more I came to terms with myself the cleaner my house became. Today I am a better mother, better wife, better friend and better housekeeper.

No, I don't enjoy cleaning, but I have learned to return things to their rightful places and clean one room thoroughly every day. I feel as if I've won some sort of victory.

More important, I am free. If you visited my home you would feel the freedom. I hope you will print this letter because I am sure there are many slobs out there who don't know why they are slobs or how to change. To all of them, I say: I did it. So can you.[5]

I want my home to say "thank you" to God. I want my home to say "you're important" to my family. I want my home to say "you're welcome" to visitors.

My mom says, "Don't spend so much time accumulating as getting rid of." The best house we lived in as kids had hardly any furniture. Maybe your possessions are taking charge of you, rather than your taking charge of them. Remember—a place for everything. . . . If there are not enough places, maybe a garage sale is in order.

Make lists. Debbi puts everything on a list—from wiping off the refrigerator door to cleaning out the hall closet. What a wonderful feeling to cross off a completed chore. If I have done something that was not on the list, I write it down and then cross it off. The more cross-offs, the better I feel—and the more convincing I can be to my husband that I haven't been eating bonbons and watching soap operas all day when he comes home and trips on a Tinker Toy.

Don't make your list just a drudge list. Put goodies on it: read to the kids, call a friend, have sauna facial over bathroom sink, and so on.

Kathy says she cleans in the morning when the kids are less likely to get on her nerves. I'm a morning person, too. Find a good time for you and your schedule.

Remember that you and your family live in this house. If you were a neat-nik before you had kids, you had better mend your ways, or the messes children make will send you right over the edge. You can't possibly enforce a rule that says "Don't touch the walls." Fingerprints are a fact of life—a blessed fact of life.

It's also hard to enforce "Don't touch Aunt Agatha's crystal sugar bowl." Many parents refuse to put breakables and heirlooms out of children's reach, because they want them to learn what the word *no* means. Personally I feel there are enough opportunities to teach the meaning of "No!" without risking the porcelain knickknacks. Perhaps a mother with only one child can keep close enough watch over the child's every action, but it's difficult to keep a thundering herd out of the family "pretties."

Keep the bathroom door closed unless you want your

toddlers to play dress-up with the toilet paper. Also keep the toilet lid down. Unfortunate accidents have occurred due to a child's natural curiosity about water.

Keep the baby's talcum powder out of reach of all the children. Not only is the mess horrendous, but it can be very dangerous to inhale the fine, powdery dust. Haven't you ever nearly choked on a powdered donut?

Keep the dishwasher door closed. It's irritating enough to find dirty plates spread from the kitchen to the living room, but even worse, a toddling child can trip into the silverware bin and be severely injured on the cutlery.

You know of kids' natural desire to play in the trash. If you can't keep it behind child-proof doors, use a step-on lid-opener trash can. Make sure sharp objects such as lids from tin cans are disposed of either in the bottom of the can or in some other container, perhaps an empty cereal box.

The list of safety-firsts could go on and on, but the point of this chapter is not safety. Many of these messes kids can get into are just plain dangerous. Help them avoid the danger.

You might call your kids "Columbus," because this is the Age of Discovery. No matter how often you've told them no, you never know when they will set sail for new worlds. Be prepared.

Make your house a basket case. Pretty decorator baskets can be used throughout the house as catchalls. Most women complain about not having enough drawer space. Hang it! A basket hung near the cooking area could hold spice mixes and Kool-Aid packages. A basket near a work area will keep scissors and tape away from the reach of kids who might cart off your supplies to never-never land. Baskets can hold in/out mail, bills, coupons, the phone book and message paper, marking pens (on top of the fridge is a good place), paper napkins, washcloths, a knitting project, magazines, photos. . . .

While accumulating a supply of baskets, use shoe

boxes as organizers. In fact, never let a shoe box out of the house. If you wrap a gift in it, tell the recipient you need the box back—well, depending on the situation. Our family's joke is a size twelve (huge) Nike shoe box that gets opened every Christmas. The recipient saves it to wrap a gift in for the next occasion. This got started with my phrase, "I need that box back!"

Watch for back-to-school sales. The cigar-type school boxes are great organizers. Make a masking-tape tab for the front of the lid so that when the lid inevitably gets pushed in, you can pull it up by the tab.

Take advantage of your children's height and enthusiasm when you clean. A shorter person (i.e., your three-year-old) is much closer to the baseboards than you are. Give the little ones a dust rag and let them do the low spots. Use the water they splash out of the tub to wash the bathroom floor. Always find something for children to do when they ask if they can help, or they'll soon stop asking.

Let them help with the laundry. Yes, that avalanche about to happen on the living-room couch. You may want to have a separate basket for each child's clothes and let them sort. Even without the baskets, let them sort—it's an important pre-reading exercise.

Simplify the laundry as much as you can. If your children of the same sex wear the same-size underwear, keep all the underwear in one drawer. Buy tube socks—several sizes of feet can wear them.

Socks are my most frustrating laundry problem. Keep a shoe box handy to toss in all the mismates. A pair will eventually show up. If it doesn't, you probably left it at Grandma's. Or, more likely, the dryer ate it. One sock solution is to put the dirty ones in the leg of an old panty hose. On washday tie the end, and the socks should not escape. I really like Nancy's attitude: "I just thank God for every dirty sock in the wash."

Donna does laundry one day a week. She makes sure,

though, that her husband and daughters have at least seven of everything.

Kay says she makes sure she always has a supply of pre-wash spray on hand. Amen!

Don't try to keep an immaculate house, but do try to have some order. Deniece Schofield suggests these basics when time (and, I might add, energy) is tight:

1. General pick-up of the house, including making beds
2. Laundry kept current
3. Well-balanced meals served regularly
4. Dishes done frequently
5. Bathrooms cleaned and straightened regularly
6. Entry areas clean and neat appearing. (This is to avoid embarrassment when the doorbell rings. It is not necessary for the well-being of the family, but it will help your peace of mind.)[6]

And you have probably heard this household hint: keep the vacuum cleaner out. If unexpected company comes, they will be comforted with the illusion that you were about to do something about the mess. But if your family uses the vacuum cleaner as a coffee table, you know you are doing something wrong!

If you are exhausted at the end of the day (What do I mean, "if"?), just make sure the milk is put away and leave the kitchen mess until morning. Your rest is very important in dealing with your little bundles of energy.

Now quit apologizing for the way your house looks. Apologizing for the mess, even if it's very little mess, draws attention to it. If your visitors don't know that children get things out faster than you can put them away, they are about to find out.

Have a plan for housework—a flexible one that allows for all the little interruptions. I sometimes envy day-care workers, although no salary in the world could entice me to work at a day-care center. They can devote all their time to the children without the distractions of laundry, dishes, and dusting.

Being somewhat organized has the added dividend of being able to spend more time concentrating on your husband and children. The people, not the house, are the top priority items.

I love my home and want to make it a pleasant place for my family. Some days it is less pleasant than other days, but I'm trying. I can live with a certain amount of clutter, so that when I fall behind, as we all inevitably do, I am not nervous about the state of my house. Although I usually have several projects going on at once, I know that they can be tucked out of sight into their proper places.

So does Roger. Every time he sees me start folding up and putting away, he says, "Oh, good! Grandma and Grandpa are coming!"

Notes

1. Deniece Schofield, *Confessions of an Organized Housewife* (Cincinnati, Ohio: Writer's Digest Books, 1982), p. 142.

2. *Ibid.*, p. 143.

3. *Ibid.*, p. 145.

4. Edith Flowers Kilgo, *Handbook for Christian Homemakers* (Grand Rapids, Michigan: Baker Book House, 1983), p. 37.

5. Ann Landers, News America Syndicate, *El Dorado Times.*

6. Schofield, op. cit, p. 48.

9

Eat Every Carrot and Pea on Your Plate

Eat Every Carrot and Pea
on Your Plate

Want a good laugh? Read any advice about feeding children. It usually goes something like this: "Tasty, nutritious food in a relaxed atmosphere makes eating a happy experience."

Take lunch at our house. *Please,* take it—to paraphrase that old joke. And take the dirty breakfast dishes still around the kitchen sink at lunchtime. And then take the children to McDonald's so I can eat my tuna salad in peace. Maybe I will even eat sitting down.

The secret to a relaxed atmosphere around mealtime is not to feed the kids at mealtime. Feed them before.

When a neighbor, mother of three grown sons, brought over a baby gift for Alex, I explained that we were getting along quite well with our three little guys, but that everything seemed to fall apart at about noon.

"Oh? Around noontime, huh?"

"Yes, we all just seem to lose our cool then."

"Right around noontime," she said again. She probably wanted to say, "Look, lady, those kids are hungry. Get them fed earlier, or at least give them a graham cracker to chew on while you're getting a meal together."

Children need snacks. Their tummies are smaller, so they can't hold as much at mealtime, but their energy needs are large. Give them something substantial to keep them going and to help make the busy-ness around food-preparation time more pleasant for everyone.

I'm sure you have your own snack repertoire, but if you are like me, you are always on the lookout for new ideas. So are the kids. Variety helps them eat without fussing.

These snacks can also be used at breakfast or lunch:

Different kinds of bread—muffins, banana bread, oatmeal bread, for example

Cinnamon toast

Bread 'n butter 'n apple butter

Bowl of cold cereal

Chunks of fruit (Let the kids dip them in honeyed yogurt for fun.)

Applesauce with red food coloring added

Applesauce Jello (Red raspberry Jello, 1 cup boiling water, 1 cup applesauce, 1 tablespoon vinegar; takes two hours to set.)

Finger gelatin blocks (Use less liquid than usual.)

Round eggs (hard-boiled and peeled)

Cheese on bread (Melt slices of cheese on bread in toaster oven, or microwave just enough that it sticks to the bread. Our kids' favorite is "white cheese on bread"—mozzarella or Monterey Jack—which they also often have for breakfast.)

American cheese slices (Let them break the cheese into triangles, squares, rectangles, or cut them with a cookie cutter.)

Animal cookies—a handful in individual bowls

Leftover breakfast pancake, waffle, or French toast

Yogurt (If you make your own, flavor it with jarred baby fruit.)

Yogurt popsicles

Jello popsicles (These won't melt! They just get a little

wobbly. Make Jello according to package instructions and freeze in molds.)

Cracker smorgasbord

Apple slices (peeled, please, for young children) spread thinly with peanut butter

Cookies with texture—oatmeal, granola

Pumpkin pie

Toast sticks

Any sandwich that has been cut with a cookie cutter (Save the scraps for bread crumbs; let them sprinkle the crumbs over casserole servings—they may be more inclined to eat something they can't see.)

Fruit cocktail—a.k.a. "Fruit cottontail" (Stock up when it's on sale; keep grapes away from the baby.)

Orange wheels (Cut the "heel" off both ends of an orange, slice through the peel from end to end, then slice orange in 1/4" circles. Kids open them up and eat out the orange.)

Milk shake made with fruit

Cup of tomato soup made with milk—toast croutons are "fish"

Scrambled eggs with cheese

Cheese ball—my favorite holiday recipe is a favorite snack at our house

Keep some snacks where each child has access to them. Otherwise they will drive you nuts wanting you to get them something to eat all the time. Bruce can find a hard-boiled egg in the fridge; Roger can get a piece of cheese. Alex, who is crawling and loves cabinets, can get a cracker from a box on the bottom shelf. (Not as "dangerous" as it sounds. The rest of the bottom cabinets are child-proof—cleansers, bug sprays, and furniture polish are elsewhere.) Unfortunately, he can also take the cereal boxes out. If I'm not watching, my next steps into the kitchen will go "crunch."

Don't give nuts or popcorn to children under three. If caught in the throat, they can expand. Also avoid raisins, olives, hard candy, and carrot sticks for kids under eighteen months. Corn, leafy vegetables, cucumbers, baked beans, chocolate, and uncooked onions are hard for young children to digest. A new report says that hot dogs are custom-made for children to choke on because of their round shape and smooth texture. If you serve franks, cut them lengthwise at least twice.

Watch the food the older children are carrying around. They might try to feed it to the baby. Mom tells of the time I was so proud that I got Tommy, my new baby brother, to stop crying. I had stuffed a cheese curl into his mouth.

Are they constantly begging for something to drink? Help make them more independent. Keep a cup with a sipper lid (Tupperware makes a good one, or use training cups)—one for each child—in the refrigerator, full of juice, milk, water, whatever. When they need a drink, they can get it. When we were kids, milk was delivered to our home in five-gallon cardboard containers with a spigot. It was wonderful to be able to get our own milk.

A thermos with a spigot, or an air pot, may also be an easy way to make drinks more available to the older children and to enable them to serve the younger ones.

Vicky color-codes the cups she hands out to her kids. Each child uses only one color. That way, she knows who to scold for not getting a cup back in the right place and who has not yet finished his or her milk.

Whatever children like today they will dump on the floor tomorrow. Put a little pizzazz into their peanut butter. Try an open-faced (and I do mean "faced") peanut-butter sandwich man. Decorate a round-cut piece of bread spread with peanut butter to look like a face, using grated cheese, apple slices, raisins, and so on. Cute, huh?

We get a lot of mileage from a pot roast. The day after it is served, I grind up the leftovers, stir some gravy with it, and heat it up for warm roast-beef sandwiches. I may use some of the ground meat for a cold sandwich spread that my kids like on bread that I've cut with a cow-shaped cookie cutter.

I never make a sandwich without asking if the child wants it in rectangles, fingers, four little-bitty squares, four tiny triangles, or one big square. If it's not according to specifications, it probably won't get eaten. It is also a good opportunity to teach shapes to the children.

Nutrition? Just say the word and you have a food fight on your hands. I've heard different experts say everything from ice cream is a nutritious snack, to grocery-store eggs are so bad for us that we'd be better off not eating them at all. What to do?

Use your own good sense and believe everything you have heard about a balanced diet, whether you are a health-food purist or a conventional consumer. Do yourself and your kids a favor by staying away from regular consumption of candy, chips, and pop. I would rather advise staying away from them altogether, but I feel that children who grow up with such things being an absolute no-no will be inclined to go hog-wild with them every chance they get later on. Many will disagree with me, I know. Donna thinks the reason her girls don't like candy is that they never have really had enough to develop a taste for it.

Our Friday-night family time is a popcorn-and-pop party. The kids don't beg for pop during the week because they know they'll get some on Friday. Mom, you're in charge. You can be very firm about saying no to sugared treats in the grocery store.

Roger's little friend Emily is the epitome of the healthy child—rosy-cheeked, bright-eyed, shiny-haired. I have never seen that child with dried you-know-what under her nose. In fact, the only times I've seen Emily dirty is when she has played with my boys. Her mom rarely has to cancel plans to stay home with a sick daughter.

Emily's mother, Marcia, is not a health-food nut, but she is very aware of nutrition. It comes from her upbringing: "My folks were so poor that we couldn't afford doctors or medicine. So my mom made sure we had very good diets, very nutritious. Goodness, I can hardly sleep at night if Emily hasn't had a fresh fruit or vegetable at least once during the day."

Making a point of getting good food into our children's tummies reinforces the biblical truth that our bodies are the temples of God (1 Cor. 3:16). Tell the kids that. And explain that "God made you beautiful and I want to take care of what God made." This kind of talk may be just the thing to help them keep away from substance abuse when they become older and are out from under your protective influence.

Healthy kids have a great deal to do with Mom's ability to cope.

Now back to that famous "relaxed atmosphere." This starts with planning and preparing ahead your big meal of the day. Breakfast and lunch are another story—every family's situation is different. Perhaps there is at least one meal a day when Mom, Dad, and the kids gather together. Because of schedules, this is not always possible, but you usually know that you will need a meal on the table at a certain time. What you don't know is that the baby will wake from his nap early and demand to be fed, that the preschooler will run off to a neighbor's house without telling you, and that the toddler will play dress-up with a roll of toilet paper. Here's Daddy, home and hungry and met not by the smells of supper cooking, but by the distinct aroma of a dirty diaper. Kathy calls the hour before Daddy comes home "the arsenic hour."

So, while the kids are napping or watching "Sesame Street," peel potatoes or brown hamburger. Prepare meals that are quickly put together after lunch and take all afternoon to crock-pot or simmer on the stove. Double the recipe for planned-overs. Have a file in your head, or taped to the inside of your kitchen cabinets, of meals that can be put together in less than half an hour. If you have a microwave, make full use of its time-saving potential.

Cooking ahead allows me to supervise table setting. Even a two-year-old—well, two-and-a-half-year-old—can help set the table. Help the child count out what needs to be put around, or get everything out, put it on a chair, and let your small assistant cart it to the table. If you need to re-set anything, do it when the little helper is not looking.

Some days it's fun to help Mom set the table. Some days it's not. Teach them now to be helpers regardless of whether they like it. Otherwise, you'll be a scullery maid to your teenagers.

After the meal, everyone can take his or her own plate to the kitchen. Even Dad. Especially Dad, since little eyes are watching for that example.

Kids will be kids at the table. This means that as soon as they sit down, the potty-trained kids will have to go to the bathroom. It's okay. Let them, without complaining. They have been playing or working so hard that they just now realized they have to go. The same thing happens to me. But remember to help them tend to business before the next mealtime.

If the baby has already eaten, set him in the dining room or kitchen with the rest of the family anyway. And turn off the TV, wherever it is located.

"Kids being kids" also means they will complain about the food and declare that they would rather eat dirt. You probably have it in stereo. Mom and Dad in the middle, a whining preschooler at one end with a protegé at the other end, encouraging each other in the symphony. Then Mom and Dad add to the chorus with "How do you know you don't like it—you haven't even tried it?" and so on.

Lighten up. The title of this chapter is a line my grandpa often used to get us to open our mouths by giggling—when we were old enough to understand the pun. Not taking the meal so seriously can help everyone relax and enjoy the food and each other.

Parents, and especially dads, can cause much stress at the table by insisting that everything on the child's plate be eaten. Perhaps too much was put on the plate in the first place—remember, their tummies are smaller. Perhaps the child gulped down a whole glass of milk before the food was served. That will fill a kid up. Perhaps a snack was a little too substantial or the child ate something earlier without the parents' knowledge. Or perhaps the little darlin' is just being stubborn.

Never force-feed. There's nothing like trying to force-feed a youngster to completely blow a chance for a relaxed atmosphere. (Exception: when Alex refuses food at the beginning of a meal, I pinch his cheeks together to get the first morsel in his mouth. He will usually gladly eat more. If not, I forget it or try again later.)

If your kids will fall for the airplane-in-the-hangar game, use it. "Here comes the airplane! Open up!" We've updated it to "space shuttle"—affectionately known as "space shovel."

Call the food by another name. Spaghetti almost always gets eaten when we call it "worms." I often use spinach spaghetti, and "little green worms" are even better. Call hot cereal "porridge"—three-bears style.

And then there's the magic fork. Load the child's fork with green beans or tuna casserole and say, "I wonder if that food will disappear." Then look away. Sure enough, it has disappeared into the child's mouth and is about to be swallowed. "Oh, my goodness! Where did that food go? I wonder if it will happen again." Yes, it happens again! Over and over. Never have we had an incident where the magic fork dumped the disappearing food on the floor. Bruce had us make up a chant: "Magic fork, magic fork, are you working? Are you working?" Look away. *Gulp.* Food is gone. Reload.

It is our custom to sing our prayer before a meal. We hold hands and sing with our eyes open, looking at each other and smiling. "We thank you, God, for this good food. For happy homes, we thank you, God. Amen." This is the prayer my family sang when I was a child. The baby loves our choir. He gets very excited when we sing and insists on holding hands.

The eyes-open rule eliminates this conversation: "Bruce had his eyes open!"—"Oh, yeah, how do you know?"

Praying while looking at each other does have a calming effect at the table. After the song, if anyone has some spontaneous words of thanks, those are offered. When all my brothers and sisters get together, we always sing our traditional chorus, which means we start the meal with a lump in our throats. This simple prayer that my parents taught us to sing at mealtime is a blessed tie that binds.

It will take a while for mealtime to be really a fun time, a time to visit, a time to laugh, a time to share joys and concerns. After all, if your oldest child is three, there's a limit to the amount of witty and sparkling conversation that can take place around the table. Even so, your table time is a time to honor the Lord.

If a regular family mealtime at least once a day is not always possible—maybe Daddy won't be home for supper when the kids need to eat—make it as much of a togetherness affair as you can. When Don is not home, it seems so much easier just to take out of the fridge whatever I think the kids will eat and put it in front of them than it is to make a real meal. The thought has occurred to me, though, "What if, for some reason, we didn't have a

90

daddy? Would we always eat 'hit and miss'? What would the kids learn about being a family?"

With or without Daddy at the table, mealtime is an important time to teach and to learn what being a family is all about.

Before anyone can eat, a trip to the grocery store is necessary. The easiest way to do this is to wait until Daddy comes home, then go alone. Mrs. Mulvaney, who raised nine children, says she didn't go to the store for over six years. She waited until her husband came home and then sent him.

Even if Don is home, I take one of the boys with me. It's some valuable one-on-one time and also helps them learn about the grown-up world.

Don't neglect a shopping trip with the baby. When Bruce was tiny, I took him everywhere with me, including the voting polls when he was ten days old. But poor Alex was three months old before he saw the inside of a grocery store. (In my part of the country that's what we call a supermarket.) Oh, he loved it! He smiled and "talked" to everyone, soaked in the colors, the piped-in music, and the compliments from the check-out personnel and the produce stocker. The store was a giant crib mobile. Although I knew how good it is for moms to get out, I had forgotten how good it is for the baby.

Sometimes, though, you can't avoid carting all the troops along. This is my observation of mothers and little ones in the grocery store: It is the mother, not the child, who makes more noise, and the mother who has only one child with her usually makes the most. Mom's yelling and carrying on always draws more attention than the child's bad behavior. I get the feeling that the mother is trying to demonstrate her control over a child who is tired, hungry, bored, or just plain rebellious.

It is with a sense of awe that I realize my biggest wit-

ness as a Christian mother may be in the grocery store. . . .
One Saturday afternoon I took Roger on his outing with
me. He didn't particularly care about going, but I had
taken Bruce all sorts of interesting places with me in the
morning, so it was Roger's turn to go, whether he wanted
to or not.

As soon as his little bottom hit the seat of the grocery
cart, he started screaming. This yelling did not stop soon.
A friend of mine walked by, chuckling with the "I'm glad
it's you and not me" look.

"You want to push this guy around a while for old
times' sake?" I asked. Her only son is now twenty-one.

"N-o-o-o," she laughed above the screaming.

That same trip, over by the canned vegetables, I en-
countered a gal with four little-bitty children. The oldest
one could not have been more than six. They were clinging
to her, hanging on to the sides of the cart, or riding in the
seat. One little guy lagged behind. "Come on, Son," she
said calmly.

"Your children are certainly well behaved," I observed
to her.

"Thank you," she replied.

Maybe the secret is taking all the kids at once. Another
time I came across a very peaceful-looking mother with
four tiny tots hanging on to the grocery cart. There were
three boys all the same height and a little girl. Two of
the boys were holding hands. I made the same observation to this mom as before: "Your children are certainly
well behaved."

"They know that if they're not, they don't get to come
with me," she explained.

My kids also seem to be better behaved when I take
them *en masse*. Maybe it's because they are paying attention to each other and are not so distracted by the sights
and sounds around them. I don't know what makes the
difference. It is, of course, a more difficult shopping trip
for me and certainly not a time to browse.

Preparation is important. Tell the children exactly what kind of behavior is expected of them. Tell them again in the parking lot: "You walk. You don't run. You stay with me. You do not scream." (My mistake in taking Roger that day was that he needed a nap.) And then offer some immediate consequences if the rules are broken. "You will have to ride in the cart"—if he's not in the cart to begin with. "I will spank you"—a quick pop on the rear end does not create a big scene and is often very effective. Do not say, "I will send you to the car." That's a consequence that cannot and should not be followed through. Do not say, "We will leave right now," unless you fully intend to do so.

Remember that TV commercial that went, "If you want to capture someone's attention, whisper"? Is a son (or daughter) of yours playing hide-and-seek in the produce department? Catch him, grasp his upper arms firmly, get down to his eye level, look him directly in the eyes, and say in a low, intense tone, "If you don't stop running around right now, I'm going to spank you right here in front of everyone." It works better than yelling, and other shoppers will be impressed with your self-control.

Using the one-two-three method in public places is also very effective. "If you're not over here next to me by the time I count to three, I will spank your bottom." Then, Mom, follow through if the warning doesn't work, and next time it will. I have rarely—and I mean rarely—had to spank a child in public.

Offering treats at the check-out stand for good behavior is not always a smart idea. Withholding the package of gum when the child has been ornery is not immediate-enough punishment. And what if one child was naughty and the other child was nice? Do you buy the well-behaved youngster a treat, with instructions not to share with a naughty brother or sister? I have, however, been known to say, "What's wrong with a bribe if it works?"

An occasional surprise treat at the end of a shopping

trip has a nice, long-run effect: "I'm so proud of the nice way you behaved. Shall we get some gum?"

If they are well behaved near the frozen-foods section, give praise right then and there: "You're being such a good boy! I'm so proud of you!" Encourage them to be good for goodness' sake—and because you would love for someone to come up to you in the store and say, "Your children are certainly well behaved!"

Practice at home going on a shopping trip. Do some role playing under the guise of "playing store." Review the rules. Remember, Mom, your Christian witness may be on the line—not from how well behaved your children are, but from how you handle yourself. A prayer in the parking lot is appropriate!

10

A Room of My Own

A Room of My Own

On December 1, the alarm clock went off for Don to get up. I woke up instead (naturally), shut off the noise, and immediately went into labor. Between contractions, I went upstairs to where four-year-old Bruce and not-quite-two-year-old Roger were sleeping. I woke Bruce.

"Time to get up, Bruce. Today is the day I go to the hospital to have the baby."

Rubbing sleep from his eyes, he propped himself up on his elbow. "But, Mom, can we still keep Roger?" Oh, my goodness—I thought I had covered all the bases. Had he been wondering all this time what we would do with the old baby if we got a new one, or was this just a spur-of-the-moment thought?

"Of course we'll keep Roger. We'll keep all our kids!"

"Oh! That's wonderful!" And he jumped up to get ready for the big day.

I am sure there have been a few times since then that Bruce wished we *had* done something with Roger. Alex is still little and cute, not in the way and bothersome like Roger. It's the perfect setup for constant fighting. I have little doubt I could stand to have a dozen preschoolers if they did not fight, pick, punch, knock, kick, bite, or otherwise harass each other. But then they wouldn't be very normal. And I am happy for a normal family, right?

When children are so close in age, especially of the same sex, there are bound to be scraps. The kids are always competing, but there are also ways to head off some of those scraps before they happen.

Never say, "We can't go to the park because of the baby," or "We can't have Matthew come and play because of the baby." Don't verbally take away a privilege "because of the baby." You can say instead, "We can go to the park later," or, "Let's have Matthew over another time." Don't give the older ones any more reasons to resent the baby than they may already have.

Occasionally defer to an older child. If the baby is crying at the same time the toddler needs you, make sure the baby is safe, then say in the toddler's hearing, "You'll just have to wait, Baby. I need to take care of your big brother." Score one for big brother.

Make sure each child has some toys that are his or her very own, and everyone should know the owner may exercise the right to share or not to share. The older child often is showered with toys and books and goodies, and the younger one gets left to pick from the hand-me-downs. Buy some toys that are just right for the younger children to enjoy now. Alert the gift-giving grandparents.

These should not be something such as building blocks or a Candy Land game that are "community property" toys, but a plaything that says, "This is my very own." At our house Roger's talking Mickey Mouse and Bugs Bunny are off limits to anyone but him. Bruce's airplane with the hand-cranked propeller is his to do with as he pleases—to share or not.

Kay says it does no good to give identical toys—one for each child—they fight over who gets to have both of them.

In addition to some toys to call "mine," each little child needs some private territory. When my sister Elaine was young, she stomped her feet and declared, "I can't wait to get married, so I can have a room of my own!" If you have more than two children, a room for each is probably not possible. Houses are not made that way anymore. But everyone needs some space to call his or her very own.

The summer Bruce turned three and Roger was a baby, we spent working on Don's parents' farm. The pear trees were producing mightily, and Bruce often asked for a cut-up pear, supposedly to be put in Grandpa's lunch box. Then he disappeared with it. We followed Bruce out behind the hay barn, where he had stacked some hay bales to make a little room just for himself. He opened his lunch box and munched on his pear, enjoying the sights and the sounds of the farm through the doorway. When he needed to, he pulled down his pants and did his business right there in the hay. No wonder there hadn't been much action from him in the bathroom in the house. This was his own private world, just for himself, where he could get away from Roger's fussing and the adults' jabbering. Let me tell you, we had a time when we came home from the farm, convincing him that "city boys don't go potty outside."

Today Bruce's own space is at the desk that Don made for him. Roger often disappears upstairs to play alone with the Lego set.

As young as he is, Alex has a favorite place on one of our couches. It's low, and he learned early to climb up on it. I often find him there with a book in his hand. In fact, Alex would love to be an only child. Other times I have found him in a variety of secluded spots, enjoying a little bit of quiet time.

Never compare the children within their hearing. Make sure they are really out of hearing distance if you must make a verbal comparison. Even then, watch how you say it. It's one thing to comment, "Tammy looks like her dad's side of the family and Sandra like her mom's." But it's quite another to say, "Tammy is sure the one who got her father's good looks."

Roger exhibited outstanding intellectual qualities at an early age. I was always bragging about him, and people always asked me how he was. Then I realized that I was bragging about Roger with Bruce right in front of me and not saying a word about Bruce's abilities. If you brag out loud about one, brag about the other one in the same breath.

When you are disciplining one child, don't let the other child help you play the role of parent. If you are scolding Sally for not picking up her toys when asked, and Sammy says to her, "Yeah, do you want a spanking?" say, "Now, Sam, this is between Sally and me. You stay out of it." As a sometimes-bossy oldest child, I was constantly being told, "Freda Ann, you stay out of this." Now I understand why.

Watch that you don't set up that older child for a lifetime of "snitching." When I was three, I had a younger brother and a baby sister. My brother was a climber. No fence could keep him in, no cabinet was too high for the conquering hero. Mom often relied on me to be her official informer. "Freda, go see what Tommy is doing and come back and tell me." They later had a hard time breaking me of being a terrible tattletale.

Poor Tom. One year we took a family camping vacation. He was eighteen, I was twenty. We kids decided to take a walk down the road one night. Every time a car drove by, I yanked Tom out of the road. Finally he yelled, "Freda! Stop mothering me!" I got the message completely, and it has made a healthful difference in our adult relationship.

Make siblings proud of each other. Give them opportunities to build each other up. Remember that verse from Romans? *Let us then pursue what makes for peace and for mutual upbuilding.* "Oh, look what the baby can do! He can stand up all by himself!" "Oh, look what Jennie drew! Isn't it beautiful?" (unless it's on the wall). "Look how fast Jill can run. Aren't we proud of her?" You'll have the kids praising each other before you even have to do the prompting. Just make sure everyone gets praised equally in front of the others. Again, never set them up for unfair competition.

When Tom started school, it was apparent that he was not going to have an easy time of it. As he progressed, my parents discovered that he had a learning disability. This was before the days when learning-disabled kids were given the help and sensitive encouragement that they needed. So here was a very bright boy who simply could not interpret correctly what he saw in print. Here was a boy making *C*'s, *D*'s and *F*'s in a family of *A* and *B* students. (I will own up to a D in geometry.) In order to save Tom's self-respect in the family, my parents enacted and enforced the rule that our grades were our personal and private business. This eliminated the "What d'ja get?" competition in the family and gave Tom the perfect excuse not to talk about his misery.

The rest brings tears to my eyes every time I think of it. The fifth-grade students were allowed to learn to play a musical instrument. Of course, a student's grades had to be high, because the musicians would leave the classroom for group instruction. Tom wanted to play the violin, but there was no way that boy's grades were high enough. A sensitive principal waived the rule for him, allowing him to learn the violin. He excelled at it. It was the one thing that saved his self-esteem and created any kind of positive self-image. Mom is sure that it kept him from being a high-school dropout.

The point is, make your children proud of each other. If you think, "Big deal! They're so young, all they care about is survival," you're wrong. And even if that were true, you are building lifelong family habits that will help make the children loyal friends when they get older.

However, no matter how many "preventative" tactics you use, the kids are going to go for the throat sometimes. Nancy says she sets limits, then lets them go at it. If the limits are broken, there are consequences to pay.

James Dobson uses these limits in his household. They may help you decide what guidelines may be needed for your family, as far as getting along with each other:

1. Neither child is allowed to make fun of the other one in a destructive way.

2. Each child's room is his private territory.

3. The older child is not permitted to tease the younger child.

4. The younger child is forbidden to harass the older child.

5. The children are not required to play with each other when they prefer to be alone or with other friends.

6. We mediate any genuine conflict as quickly as possible, being careful to show impartiality and extreme fairness.[1]

Dobson adds that this plan requires children's respect for leadership of the parent, willingness by the parent to mediate, and occasional reinforcement or punishment.

Sometimes it is best to let them have their little quarrels on their own. They must learn to reach a conclusion. However, if it appears that they will not resolve the problem without someone getting hurt, you'd better get in there and fight for "truth, justice, and the American way."

Now consider the word *genuine* that Dobson used in point six. One evening when I was in the bathroom, I heard the most awful screaming and yelling coming from upstairs. Roger and Bruce were at it again. Roger was screaming, "Stop that, Bruce! Leave me alone! Quit it! [and so on]."

I said to myself, "This time I'm going to stay out of it. I can't be involved in every fight they have. I'm just going to hope Roger can learn to defend himself and that they can work it out on their own." The yelling got worse. I stormed out of the bathroom, ready to give Bruce the spanking of his life, and there he was, lying peacefully on the family-room floor and watching TV. I tiptoed upstairs and found

Roger playing with Legos in a monologue of this imaginary fight with Bruce.

After that I have watched Roger more closely when the actual screaming and fussing begins and discovered that while he may be provoked, he also overreacts. That gets me off Bruce's back a little bit. Since I don't have to blame him for being the big bully all the time, I don't constantly use his name when I am scolding for a fight. I can use Roger's name once in a while—"Roger, quit screaming."

Separate the fighters. This is a nice thing about young children. You can pick them up and move them to where you want them. This never works quite right for me. When I send Bruce upstairs for hassling Roger, Roger cries for Bruce to be allowed downstairs.

Instead of automatically assuming things and accusing the older child of making the younger one cry, ask the older child, "Why is Susie crying?" If the younger child happens to be playing with a toy that belongs to an older sibling, use that opportunity to teach the older child to trade for it, not grab it away. Also point out to the younger child, on an appropriate level of understanding, the principle of the rights of others to their own possessions.

Assign each child a corner of the room and tell them they must receive the other's permission before leaving their corner. Or give each of them a chore to do in a different room—dusting or cleaning off windows, washing the front of the fridge—anything with a spray bottle and a cloth is "fun," but you may need to supervise this operation.

They probably can't have a knock-down-drag-out with the baby, but the baby needs protection anyway. When you take a shower, take the baby with you into the bathroom. You might even need to take two kids with you, just to make sure they don't hurt each other.

Soon the baby is old enough to pull hair, hit brother or sister in the face with a rattle, or kick over a project an older child is working on. You can't discipline the baby, because an infant doesn't know any better. For the sake of the offended older child, who wonders why this cute little intruder gets away with everything, tell the baby "No, no. Don't do that," and try to explain to the older one that the baby is still too young to know any better, but that he or she can help Baby learn. (Good luck with that part!)

We have our share of sibling fights, but we also have our share of sibling love. The boys are affectionate among themselves, something that we encourage and set an example for in the family circle. We want them to be as proud to have each other as we are to have them.

When I came home from the hospital after Alex was born, I was sure the boys would run out to greet me with hugs and kisses and tell me how much they missed me. They were, indeed, waiting at the door with Grandma and Grandpa, but there were no screams of "Mommy! Mommy!" Instead, in the cold of December, little Roger dashed outside with his arms outstretched, screaming at the top of his lungs, "Alex! Alex!" Welcome home, little brother.

Note

1. James Dobson, *Dr. Dobson Answers Your Questions* (Wheaton, Ill.: Tyndale, 1982), p. 223.

11

Early-Childhood Experience—
Are You Kidding?

Early-Childhood Experience—
Are You Kidding?

Every once in a while I envy mothers with only one preschooler. These women, blessed with one free hand, can take their tot to story hour at the library or to museums, exhibits, and craft fairs. They can go to the city pool and not get dizzy and cross-eyed from trying to keep track of the kids. They can sit at the kitchen table making Play-Doh creations without worrying that "little britches" is under the table and eating the crumbs that fall to the floor.

A mother of one child can cart her little one all over town to music lessons, gymnastics class, dance class, swimming lessons, and preschool—all those goodies the experts say "broaden a child's experience."

I'm sure you've noticed that there are many things that you cannot easily participate in with your children—because you cannot possibly physically maneuver all these little ones and cannot afford a baby-sitter every time something comes along that one of the children would enjoy. You have probably felt some occasional guilt because of this.

Educators say that a rich early-childhood experience most readies a child for learning to read. It builds their working vocabulary. This is one reason I always try to take at least one child to the store with me or on errands. As Verletta says, many teachable moments occur when you are out of the house and away from distractions: "Don't let having a lot of kids deter learning experiences."

You have an opportunity for built-in experiences just because you have a lot of kids. What a stimulating environment! Masuru Ibuka, in the thought-provoking book *Kindergarten Is Too Late!* says:

> Many men born in poor homes make something special of themselves and this may well be accounted for by the fact that a child is likely to grow up to be superior in both character and ability if brought up in a scintillating home where the more brothers and sisters there are, the more stimulated each becomes.[1]

I told you about Mrs. Mulvaney, who avoided going to the store for six years. Her nine children did not go either. The kids also did not play out and about in the neighborhood because, she says, she just couldn't keep track of them all for their safety. Yet nearly all of these children are super-achievers in school. They have earned college scholarships. They have technical, scientific jobs. Several are very athletic and/or artistic. These children had the "scintillating" company of each other, and they had a mom who spent time with them.

There seems to be a great debate going on among early-childhood educators about whether or not to really push a very young child's intellectual ability. I refuse to feel guilty for not turning my home into the Briggs Academy for Teaching Babies to Read. But I should feel guilty if I am not using this precious time while they are young to help develop a potential for learning that they will never again have.

The best advice along this line came to me from Don's brother's wife, Elly. When Bruce was born, she said, "talk to him."

When you are changing a diaper, tell the baby what you

are doing. "Here's the changing table—oh, my! So wet! Here comes the powder. It's so soft and white. . . ."

Planning an outing? "Now we're going to the store. Oh, there are all kinds of good things to eat at the store. Let's get in the car. . . ."

So what if Baby is one week old and can't understand a word you're saying? Infants get important verbal contact and stimulation from Mother or Dad and learn about security from the parental voice. Feeling secure is another thing that is very important to a child's intellectual development.

Joy's eight-year-old son said to her, "You know, Mom, I really appreciate that you tell me things. You always explain what we're doing." Joy had long been in that habit, and Matt is a secure, creative boy.

A child's point of view in the adult world of language was illustrated to me so clearly the summer I spent in Finland. Nearly everyone in Finland learns English in school, but Finns are a very shy and reserved people, and many seemed reluctant to use English. I remember having a Finnish-English argument with a bus driver over the amount of my fare. He wanted more, and I knew I had not paid that much the last time I rode. Finally a brave Finn spoke up and explained to me that the price doubles after midnight. (I don't remember what I was doing out after midnight, but I do remember that it was light outside— the midnight sun.)

The family I stayed with was very warm and friendly and spoke English with me. Indeed, it was my job to help them with their English. But when we were with friends of the family or traveling, I was often at a loss to know what was going on. Where are we going? What is going to happen next? Are they talking about lunch yet? I felt very childish. Ah-ha! This must be what a child feels like in the adult world. No wonder children behave like children!

One family we visited made it a point to speak English

whenever I was around, even if they were not talking to me. It made me feel important. It allowed me to participate. It helped me learn.

I was understanding sentences in Finnish while I had only a small vocabulary of words I could speak. Have you figured out by now that your eighteen-month-old can understand everything you are talking about? Talk to those kids! Talk and talk!

I love going places and explaining things to the children. It enlarges their world while it allows me to see the world through fresh eyes. In the car, talk about good driving habits—why you turn the signal on; red means "stop"; talk about the shapes of the signs. Tell them the names of the streets you are on, the names of shopping centers, the colors of the cars you park beside. You may be like the gal in a carload of women who forgot that she was not with her children and pointed to the sky, "Oh, lookie! Airplane!"

How did parents ever teach their children anything before the advent of preschool and "Sesame Street"? They talked to them. Margaret Jensen, in the delightful book *First We Have Coffee,* describes the education she and her brother and sisters received as their mother went about her daily tasks:

> As Mama ironed, she taught. Her methods were simple: Endless songs and stories and Bible verses for us to memorize. . . .
> Ironing days were full of talk. Childish problems and questions were discussed in this classroom disguised as Mama's kitchen.[2]

Teach about the facts of everyday life. "Here are five plates for supper. One-two-three-four-five. If we had one more, that would be six. Five plus one is six." "Let's count the diapers on the clothesline." "Here's a pretty green leaf. Here's one like it, but it is yellow."

Hand in hand with talking to them is reading to them. Nancy S. says that when her older children were young, she was not in the habit of reading to them. With the younger ones, she started reading and can tell by their schoolwork that reading has made a difference.

When you are feeding the baby, cuddle the other kids next to you on the couch and read anything from *The Cat in the Hat* to the *World Book Encyclopedia*.

Turn off the TV and read to them. Let the housework go and read to them. Delay their bedtime and read to them. Let the "clutter" in your house be books, newspapers, and magazines. Few people will think you're a bad housekeeper. Most will think you're a good mother.

My mother is a Chapter I teacher in a public school. This is just the fancy government name for a special teacher who takes out of the classroom any kids who are having trouble with reading or math and gives them extra help.

Parents occasionally ask her, "What can I do to help my child?" When Mom suggests that they spend as little as ten minutes a day reading with the youngster, the reaction is, "Oh, I don't have time!"

John Rosemond, in his syndicated column "What's a Parent to Do?" says that a child is never too young to be read to.

Early reading stimulates language development as well as cognitive growth. In addition, studies have shown that as a child's communication skills improve, so does motor coordination.

The nurturing that takes place when a parent reads to a child helps strengthen the child's sense of security, which, in turn, contributes greatly to the later development of independence.

Security, independence and mastery—these are the ingredients that go into the making of good self-esteem.[3]

I believe that next to leading our children to God, the

most important thing we can do as parents is give them a healthy sense of self-worth.

Did you have hobbies and pastimes before you got married and had kids? Where are those hobbies and pastimes now? Don't give them up just because you have children who demand so much of you. Your special activities and interests are creative learning experiences for them—provided your hobby is not knife throwing or sword swallowing. You may need to make some adjustments in the time you spend on them, or the goals you set for having projects completed, or where your tools and equipment are kept. But don't give up the skills you have developed.

I never realized how important a special hobby or interest is to women (especially stay-at-home moms) until I overheard one woman talk about winning a prize in a fabric-painting competition. "I was so proud!" she exclaimed. "I just wanted to stand up and say, 'Hey! I made that!'"

A hobby can build up your self-esteem. Unlike housework, where no promotions are given nor prizes awarded for good work, a hobby is something of your very own. You can see when improvement has taken place. People will "ooh" and "ahh" over clothes you make for the kids and yourself, but no one will tell you what a lovely job you did waxing the floor.

A hobby or special interest will give you something to talk about other than how many times Junior made it to the potty. If you do not have a pastime or special projects, get some. If you already have some, develop them.

Your children benefit from your interests and hobbies. If my working was good for my kids at all, it was because it gave them the idea that Mommy was also a person who had interests and skills other than Mommy-ing. The children learn from and about things you do, if you let them watch and participate as much as possible.

111

Bruce was almost four when Don built the addition to our house. Baby #3 was on the way, and this family addition called for increasing our living space as well. Bruce helped Don hammer nails and measure and did quite a good job of it. In fact, he was so intent on helping Don that I was beginning to feel left out. Oh, well, I had just discovered the joy of quilting and was busy learning about my new hobby.

One afternoon Bruce left the hammer and nails and came in to announce, "I want to make a quilt, Mommy." I was "in" again! I brought out brightly colored scraps and made a square cardboard pattern. He drew around the pattern; I cut out the pieces. At the sewing machine, Bruce worked the foot-feed while I yelled "go" and "stop." He wanted to make the resulting orange and yellow rectangle into a pillow. I cut out the backing; we sewed around its sides; he stuffed it; then I showed him how to hold a needle and thread to sew up the opening. He worked so hard and so diligently. The project took several days.

The last stitch was barely in when Bruce announced, "I'm going to give this to Roger, 'cause it's little and so is he." And he proudly presented it to his little brother. Not a dry eye in the house.

Let them learn about cooking, gardening, music, sports, nature, sewing, painting. Give them an activity that is a child-size equivalent of what you are doing. When Debbi paints, she puts her boys at a table with watercolors. If music is your thing, buy the children toy instruments and a child's music-lesson book. Don loves basketball, and Bruce helped him build a child-size hoop in the back yard. We found a used typewriter for Roger at a garage sale so he wouldn't constantly beg to use mine. Let them dump the flour in the cookie dough and help plan meals. Make a garden plot for each child to tend. Look at picture books of your hobby with them. And always talk about what you are doing.

You have probably figured this out about toys: the more

"educational" they are, the more pieces they have. Let the grandparents buy the educational toys (and keep them at their house to play with), and you concentrate on what you already have at home.

Talk about shapes and sizes. "The front door is a rectangle. The car wheel is round. Is it bigger than your tricycle wheel?"

Match colors. Match the socks (if you're lucky). "Look, you're wearing matching shirts today. They are both red."

Tell your kids about their extended family. Tell them the grandparents' first names. Tell them that Aunt Lisa is Mommy's sister. Our kids never tire of looking through our family photo albums and baby books. Yes, do try valiantly to keep a baby book for each child, so that in later years you don't have to tell your youngest child that his or her baby book got lost in a flood.

Don't call things "whatchamacallits" or "thingamajigs." Say, "Please get the dishrag in the second drawer on the left." Then show the child how to find that drawer.

In the store, assign each kid a small verbal "list" of items to look for. Have one count out five apples to put in the bag, another pluck the family's favorite cereal from the shelf. Keep them with you, though—no unsupervised scavenger hunts!

Spell words as you say them. "Looks like you need a c-o-a-t today. Do you know what c-o-a-t spells? It spells coat!"

Give tasks with several steps involved. Set up "learning centers." There may be a craft center for coloring and painting (disguised as the kitchen table), a music center for listening to the record and tape player, a reading center near the book bins, with overstuffed pillows and beanbag chairs to sit on—one for each child or there will be fighting.

Listen for sounds. B-r-r-r-r-m. "That sounds like a motorcycle." "Do you hear that bird outside?" This can lead naturally into taking advantage of the children's natural inclination toward rhythm and music. Make up a little tune to learn the days of the week, phone number, address, whatever. Children delight in reading or hearing poems and making up chants and verses. That last bit is not hard. For example, Roger and I sat out in the swing in the backyard one day and made up a chanting song about our neighborhood: "We have a gray house, tra-la-la-la-la. Joyce has a yellow house, tra-la-la-la-la. Kelli has a white house, tra-la-la-la-la. We like our houses, tra-la-la-la-la."

Preschool is a wonderful invention. If you can send a child to preschool two mornings a week, you have that time to concentrate on the other children, and the little student has a special and unique experience.

But preschool is not absolutely necessary for a child's academic development. Examine your motives for sending a child to such a program. Many parents use preschool as a substitute for paying personal attention to their offspring's intellectual development.

Recognize the differences in each of your children. One child may want to read by the age of three; one may not even be interested in holding a pencil until kindergarten. Give encouragement and praise to each child for whatever he or she can do.

Early-childhood experience? You may feel as if you are the one getting all the experience. Even though you may not be able to get out and about as much as you would like, you can create rich experiences for your children as you allow them to participate in your world and in the world around them.

Notes

1. Masaru Ibuka, *Kindergarten Is Too Late!* (New York: Fireside Books, 1977), p. 86.

2. Margaret Jensen, *First We Have Coffee* (San Bernardino, Calif.: Here's Life Publishers, Inc., 1982), pp. 36, 37.

3. John Rosemond, in a nationally syndicated parenting column.

12

The Daddy You Married

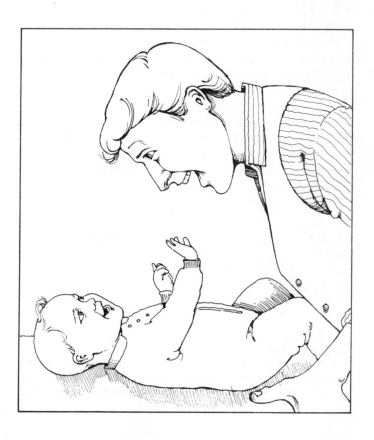

The Daddy You Married

My husband coaches eighth-grade basketball. When Alex was tiny, I enjoyed taking the kids to the home games. The middle school was one of the few places we could go that did not require crossing a street or parking lot to get into the building.

This last basketball season, my piano-lesson schedule was back in full swing, so we couldn't attend the games. Don would come home after the games with horror stories of his team's playing. He could barely mumble the final score. Don didn't mind losing the games as much as he minded the attitude of the kids—that he didn't seem to be able to make them care whether or not they played their best.

One afternoon I had a piano lesson cancellation, so I loaded up the boys and headed for the game. We sat through a humiliating first half. As we watched the score for the other team pile up, one of Don's fellow teachers leaned over to me and said with a chuckle, "I hope you have Don's favorite meal cooking." This was a middle-aged man with two grown daughters, so I assumed he spoke from experience.

The boys and I left early. I fed the kids, cleared off the dining-room table, and set two places with the good dishes. We were having the plain, ordinary roast that I fix about once a week.

Don came home with that familiar gray look on his face that says, "Don't even ask." He greeted the boys, then I plopped them down in front of the TV without guilt.

Don and I had a nice, quiet meal together. He raved over the roast. Sitting back and sighing, he said, "Thanks. That's the best thing that has happened to me all day."

So often I neglect my husband's needs. I practically lie in wait for him at the door, ready to pounce, so I can tell him whose nose to wipe, or who should be handed a graham cracker, or that the tricycle needs fixing immediately. But this man I married wasn't always Daddy. Sometimes I forget that.

My husband is a wonderful father. A terrific daddy. I often tease him that he is a better mother than I am. He's very patient with the kids and does a better job with the laundry than I do.

Debbi's husband, Gary, is so good at helping out that he doesn't consider it "helping," but part of the responsibility of being a parent. As the father of four little ones, he is aware of the pressures on his wife and takes his share of the responsibility seriously.

When a baby arrives, some men don't help out as much as we need them to because they're afraid of how tiny that newborn looks. Is it time for a lesson at your house to help him get over that fear? You may have noticed, though, that with each baby he got better at handling an infant. Or maybe he's good about giving the older children special help and attention while you concern yourself with the baby.

Another reason some men don't help out as much as we need them to is that their wives criticize them when they do. Shame on those wives! Here's when you can treat your husband as you would treat kids to whom you are trying to teach responsibility. You wouldn't scold them for putting forks on the wrong side of the plate. You would praise them for helping to set the table. Thank your husband for doing the laundry. Explain at a more romantic moment that the colored clothes don't usually go in hot water with the diapers.

Some women think they should never have to thank their husbands for doing household chores. After all, he lives there, too. If you mowed the lawn or did some other job that he usually does, would you want it to go unnoticed? Would you feel like doing it ever again if nothing positive was said about it? Thank your husband for vacuuming the floor. Be gracious about any assistance you get.

Some husbands do not deal with diapers well. I know of one husband who will not stay with the children in the evening, so his wife can go out, because he's afraid it means changing a dirty diaper. Keep a pair of rubber gloves next to the toilet at all times. Even the smell does not seem as bad with rubber gloves on the hands. Your baby-sitter will appreciate this, and so will your own hands. Keep air-freshener in the bathroom and near the changing table. Give the sensitive dad a break.

I'll never forget one of the most heroic things my dad did for me. I was nine or ten years old and was left in charge of my toddler brother for a short time one afternoon. He had been taking a nap and, lo and behold, woke up with a dirty diaper. The problem was, he somehow missed the diaper and the mess was simply all over the bedroom. I called my dad, who was working in his office at the church. He dropped everything and came straight home to help me deal with the mess. What a dad!

Perhaps some dads would help more if they simply knew exactly what to do. Would you know how to help your husband if you showed up at his place of business ready for action? You'd have to get some instructions. Maybe it's time for a heart-to-heart: "If you would feed the baby and keep the kids away from me while I am getting supper ready, I think our whole evening would go a lot smoother." Or, "You know, the best way you can help me is by giving the kids their baths at night. I'm so exhausted by the end of the day. It would be a treat for them, too." Then suggest that you wouldn't be nearly so tired when you got into bed.

There are also men who rarely saw their own fathers with their hands in the dishwater. Or maybe their mothers waited on the male family members hand and foot. Our brother-in-law, Clay, is the best all-round house helper I know. He grew up in a family of five boys, but: "Everyone had a chance to be 'Susie.'" Don't blame your mother-in-law if your husband doesn't know what to do with a broom. But be sensitive to the way he did learn responsibilities in the home.

Some husbands don't help enough to suit us because they cannot hear their nagging wives. They tune them out. Nagging never got a job done without resentment. "It is better to live in a desert land than with a contentious and fretful woman" (Prov. 21:19).

Encourage Dad to take one or more kids with him on his own errands. Then make it easier for him by sending along a container of Wet Wipes and a package of graham crackers. Remind him that there are clean training pants in the glove compartment.

Several times I've seen Kay's husband, Wayne, in the grocery store with his two tiny sons hanging on to the cart. I picture Kay at home enjoying special time with their daughter, or both of them taking a nap.

Even kids in diapers revel in outings with Dad. And Dad goes exciting places Mom does not—the lumberyard, the dump, the hardware store. I know my boys get tired of being dragged through the fabric section of TG&Y. Donna's husband, Randy, has a very special relationship with their young daughters (almost to the exclusion of Donna) because he lets them participate in everything he does, from woodworking to building a dune buggy.

119

Then there's Connie's husband, Cayetano. He says, "I wonder if I'm weird or something because I love to hold and rock the baby." Weird, no. Wonderful, yes! This man also likes to baby-sit his kids and Connie's friends' kids, so Connie can get out of the house with "the girls." And when the baby wakes up in the middle of the night and Connie says, "If I don't get my sleep, I'll be sick tomorrow," Cay knows she means it and gets up to tend to little Carmen.

Let your husband know that you need him. He is the father of these children. Encourage him to participate in all that he can. These young years with their fathers are very important to children. They are learning that God is their heavenly Father and that their earthly father is God's special messenger.

The terrible irony about dads and their families of young children is that this time period, when Mom and the family need him most, is also when a man needs most to "hustle" in the business world. His career may now require more of his time and attention than ever. He may even need to take an additional part-time job to keep up with the demands of his growing family.

Be sensitive to the financial pressures facing your husband. You may not be able to be like the woman in Proverbs 31 who "considers a field and buys it" (v. 16), but you can clip coupons, shop for bargains, recycle hand-me-downs, buy bread at the day-old bakery. In short, you can demonstrate to your husband that you are being a good steward of the money he works so hard for.

Trouble with family finances when the children are young is a cause of strife in many marriages. I know of a family with four youngsters. The father makes a good salary at his job. Yet they are spending money faster than he can make it. They had to sell a lovely home and move into cheaper, rented accommodations. There is tension between the couple, but he refuses to get some good, solid financial counseling. It is a matter of pride that keeps him from laying all of his money cards on the table. He would rather start over in a different city than face up to their present situation and straighten out the mess they are in.

Mom, help Dad deal with the financial realities of raising his family. He will appreciate it. Also help your husband step out on faith in financial matters.

When I quit my job as a teacher, Don took on double and triple duty. He got up at 5:00 A.M. to throw a paper route. He taught school, coached basketball, came home after school or practices to leave again for house painting and carpentry jobs. Thursday evenings he worked at the city library. Both Bruce's and Roger's first sentence was "Daddy's at work."

It was a step out on faith, just as when I quit my job, that he gave up the library job and the paper route soon after. We're a lot more relaxed around here these days.

In addition we have been giving over and above our tithe for most of our married life. Everything you've heard about tithing is true—the more you give the less you miss it. You can't out-give the Lord. I know many, many couples who say tithing has been such a blessing to them in their marriages.

Don't let being a parent cause you to neglect your marriage. Judy, mother of four, says you can't afford not to have a "date" with your husband once a month. Linda's sister kept their three children overnight, so Linda and her husband could have a getting-to-know-you weekend at a motel in a nearby big city.

Bruce and Roger spent a week at my parents' house this summer. It was noontime of the first day they were gone. Alex was down for a nap, and Don had come home for lunch. There was no spilled milk, no one whining because he didn't like what was being served and refused to eat it, no screen doors banging, no one jumping off a chair to go to the bathroom. I placed a chicken-salad sandwich in front of Don, complete with lettuce and sliced tomatoes. I

121

put one at my place, then sat down across from him. We just looked at each other. Both of us burst into laughter and at the same time said, "Who are you?"

Suddenly, Daddy was "Don." I had become so involved with my role as a parent that I was shocked to be reminded that this man I share my house with is my husband! I felt as if I needed a refresher course in being a wife.

Bonnie Trude, in her book *A Woman More Precious Than Jewels*, says,

> After marriage a woman usually becomes too busy and too mentally occupied with herself, her children, her home, her husband's problems, etc. to notice anything about her husband to genuinely praise and appreciate. And even when she does mentally acknowledge his "good points," she often takes him for granted and fails to communicate to her husband the respect and gratitude she ought to have for him (Eph. 5:33).[1]

Good advice about marriage that I've so often used comes from Marabel Morgan's *The Total Woman*. Basically it is the four A's—Accept him. Admire him. Adapt to him. Appreciate him.[2] That episode at lunch without the children caused me to review those principles.

It had to be the Lord who finally got Don and me together, because our stormy courtship didn't give us much of a chance. We broke the engagement twice. The problem? My unwillingness to accept absolutely everything about this man that I loved. When I realized the problem was mine and not his, we were able to make a go of it. No more nagging, no more put-downs, no more sarcastic remarks. Learning to accept—totally and truly—has kept our relationship growing year after year.

Accept him. God accepts us just as we are. We must be willing to have that attitude toward our husband, our children, our parents, our friends, and toward ourselves.

Admire him. Use words. Say them "loud and clear." Children glimmer, glow, and grow with praise. So does your husband. "I've always loved the sparkle in your eyes." (Who cares whether your man is fat and bald, if his eyes sparkle?) "Your ability to take an engine apart and put it back together again amazes me." "You are so calm and patient with the kids—I always feel more relaxed when you're home."

Brag about him to other people. Show your pride about him to the kids. "Your daddy's so thoughtful of others." "Daddy works so hard for us." "Don't we have a handsome Daddy?"

Adapt—that's the biggie. That famous verse in Ephesians 5:22—the topic of whole chapters of books, entire books, and weeks and weeks of discussion and debate in women's Bible studies—simply states, "Wives, be subject to your husbands. . . ." The submissive wife. Another version states it this way: "wives, fit in with your husband's plans." I like that one.

I am not going to elaborate on this commandment from God other than to say, "Don't knock it until you've tried it." If the idea of submission in a marriage bothers you, read on a few verses and see what God commands of husbands.

Appreciate him—the final *A*. Thank your husband for being a good provider. Thank him for mowing the lawn, taking out the garbage, changing a light bulb. Who cares if he never thanks you for washing the dishes or doing another load of diapers? Expressing appreciation is another way of giving praise. It will let him know that just because you are so busy caring for the children, you are not too busy to notice him.

And the more you let him know that he is noticed in a positive way—the more *you* will be noticed in a positive way.

Now remember, Mom, your dear husband may be as overwhelmed as you are to find himself with the responsibilities of leading, protecting, and providing for a family that has grown rather rapidly in number. Being a man, he may not yet be willing or even able to express his feelings about his role. Help him to do so (without nagging). Learn to lean on each other. And remind him that Matthew 11:28 is for the weary father as well as the weary mother: "Come unto me, all who labor and are heavy laden, and I will give you rest."

Notes

1. Bonnie Trude, *A Woman More Precious Than Jewels* (Minneapolis: The Greater Minneapolis Association of Evangelicals) Lesson 5, p. 1.

2. Marabel Morgan, *The Total Woman* (New York: Pocket Books, 1975), pp. 51–105.

13

God's Perfect Timing

God's Perfect Timing

I dread the spring of the year because that means summer is not far behind. Summer in Kansas is an unpleasant combination of heat and humidity—a mix that can make even the most patient of mothers turn into Attila the Hun.

This year I decided I would meet summer head-on. I would not complain about the heat; I would not feel guilty for the lack of freshly baked cookies in the cookie jar; I would not vacuum the floors after 10:00 A.M. And I would ask the Lord to help me through the summer.

Do you know what? It's July now. I'm sitting at the typewriter with a jacket on. So far this year, we haven't used the air-conditioner, and Don has not yet come home for lunch to find me screaming in the middle of the kitchen. Praise the Lord!

It was that conscious, willful decision, along with the Lord's help, that is getting me through the summer. I have learned that I need not let external factors control me.

And it's going to be that same conscious, willful decision, along with the Lord's help, that will get me through the remaining months of summer and into fall and winter. I am going to need a good attitude. We just found out that another baby is on the way!

I cried. Oh, I cried. It was not that we wouldn't want four children, but now, Lord? Our "plan" was to wait until Alex was four or five, then reevaluate our position. But now, Lord?

Do you know how many straight years of diapers you

126

are asking me to do? Do you know how sick I am of slacks with stretch panels and tent-shaped dresses? Besides, we already gave away the playpen and the baby swing.

The text of the pastor's sermon the Sunday after my pregnancy was confirmed was Isaiah 55:8–9:

> For my thoughts are not your thoughts, neither are your ways my ways, says the Lord. For as the heavens are higher than the earth, so are my ways higher than your ways and my thoughts than your thoughts.

The pastor mentioned something about "God's wild ideas." I nearly jumped out of my choir robe. I was able to thank God for his perfect timing in my life.

I know that at this time in your life—when you would love to go for just five minutes without hearing "Mommy!"—it seems almost cruel to say that these years while your children are so young go by so quickly. Yet knowing that keeps me going.

When I am at the "scream door," I realize that in four years there will be another presidential election. The last one seemed like only yesterday. In four years the baby we don't even have yet will be older than the baby we do have. Oh, my, I almost get teary-eyed from nostalgia over events that have not even happened yet. Putting the present in the past makes me understand how wonderful it is to be at this stage right now with my children.

Instead of a reaction ranging from shock to dismay, as it did when I announced the impending birth of our third child, the response of friends and acquaintances has been marvelously supportive. Perhaps people think a third child is an accident meriting sympathy, but a fourth child is truly God's will.

An observation. If you become pregnant or are now in such a condition, assure the older child or children that when the new baby comes, the old baby will stay. I told of Bruce's concern when I went to the hospital to have Alex. This time around, when I told Roger that we would have a new baby, he immediately asked, "Well, will Alex still live here?" For two days I assured and re-assured him that all of our kids are staying—that we would have four kids instead of three. One morning I heard him tell Alex, "Guess what, Alex—we're getting a new baby and you can stay!"

Another observation. I feel better with this pregnancy than with any of the others. I attribute that to exercise, vitamins, and relying on the Lord. Both Don and I feel that we are drawing strength from the Lord that we would not otherwise have known.

I'm making plans to relinquish certain activities and responsibilities. That includes giving up teaching piano—relying more on the Lord to meet our financial needs.

This is not a good year to be room mother or in charge of the PTA chili supper. Debbi and I have different ideas about that sort of thing. She decided that just because she has four kids, she's not going to let that keep her from being room mother and totally involved in her oldest son's school activities. My thinking is that I will have plenty of years to be room mother. I'm going to sit this one out, but will be involved in Bruce's education as much as I can without having to hire a baby-sitter.

I will not give up writing and sewing. Both are survival tactics, for different reasons.

I am encouraging independence in the boys and trying to make it easier for them to do things for themselves. Unless they are very tired, I say, "No, you do that yourself. I will not do something for you that I know you can do for yourself and have seen you do for yourself."

And—I'm preparing a garage sale. A big one, so I can get rid of, sort out, and throw away a lot of potential clutter.

One last word, Mom. Unless you've done something "permanent" (and even then, the unlikely has been known to occur), hang on to those maternity clothes.

Postscript: Catherine was born February 21, 1985.